BRIGHT

D0491364

NEW IDEAS

Wet
Playtimes

ST012983

CORNWALL COLLEGE

AGES 5-11

Deborah Sharpe

Learning Services	
Cornwall College St Austell	
Class	372·133 SHA
Barcode	ST012983
Date	18/10/07 Centre JKH 4

Author
Deborah Sharpe
All Deborah Sharpe stories and poems previously unpublished.

Editor
Christine Harvey

Assistant Editor
Margaret Eaton

Project Editor
Wendy Tse

Series designer
Joy Monkhouse

Designer
Helen Taylor

Illustrations
Baz Rowell

Cover photographs
Courtesy of Brollies Galore (www.brolliesgalore.co.uk)

Published by Scholastic Ltd,
Villiers House,
Clarendon Avenue,
Leamington Spa,
Warwickshire
CV32 5PR

Printed by Bell & Bain Ltd, Glasgow
Text © Deborah Sharpe 2005

1 2 3 4 5 6 7 8 9 0   5 6 7 8 9 0 1 2 3 4

Visit our website at www.scholastic.co.uk

British Library Cataloguing-in-Publication Data
A catalogue record for this book is available from
the British Library.

ISBN 0-439-97176-4
ISBN 978-0439-97176-8

The right of Deborah Sharpe to be identified as the Author of this work has been asserted by her in
accordance with the Copyright, Designs and Patents Act 1988.

All rights reserved. This book is sold subject to the condition that it shall not, by way of trade or otherwise,
be lent, hired out or otherwise circulated without the publisher's prior consent in any form of binding or
cover other than that in which it is published and without a similar condition, including this condition,
being imposed upon the subsequent purchaser.

No part of this publication may be reproduced, stored in a retrieval system, or transmitted, in any form or
by any means, electronic, mechanical, photocopying, recording or otherwise, without the prior permission
of the publisher. This book remains copyright, although permission is granted to copy those pages marked
'photocopiable' for classroom distribution and use only in the school which has purchased the book
or by the teacher who has purchased the book and in accordance with the CLA licensing agreement.
Photocopying permission is given for purchasers only and not for borrowers of books from any lending
service.

Contents

Introduction

Playtime allows children to take a break from their work, and to laugh and play with their friends so that they return to their studies refreshed. However, when it rains they can feel as though they've not had a break, and this may affect their behaviour, concentration and mood for the rest of the day. This book contains enough games and activities to ensure children have fun for weeks of wet playtimes, and soon your children will agree with the boy who said: 'I used to hate the rain, but now it feels like we've had playtimes even if we've been in all day!'

Resourcing wet playtimes

A handy addition to any classroom is a wet playtime box, which will ensure a resource of easily accessible equipment. The box could include: this book, a timer or stopwatch, blindfolds, a bag or container, assorted coins, a torch, a rope, wool, cotton, balloons, paper fasteners and newspaper. Usual classroom equipment like sticky tape and colouring pencils will also be needed.

Teachers, teaching assistants, lunchtime assistants and students can run the activities, and they may sometimes wish to appoint a play leader from amongst the children. Throughout the book, whoever is running the game is referred to as the 'play leader'.

Most of the games require a child to take a lead role, and this player is referred to as 'It'. The fairest way to pick someone to be 'It' is to choose the first to answer a simple question – for example, *Tell me something beginning with 'B'*.

Conducting the play

Some children may need time before they commit themselves to playing a game, and the play leader might need to encourage them to join in. However, it is important that the children have the choice, as they would if they were playing outside.

Children with special needs might need another child to be their game buddy. Allow the two to play as one player so that the game buddy provides what the other lacks. You might also even things up by giving children with special needs more time or a head start. Alternatively, they could be the play leader.

The 'Ground rules' in the activities are essential to help everybody play fairly and enjoy the games. Emphasise that if children do not follow the ground rules they must sit out of the game for a period of time.

Encouraging positive behaviour is the best way to ensure that all children have a good time. At the end of the session the teacher or play leader could nominate someone as 'Best player'. This should be the child who played fairly, was kind to others and was cheerful, even if losing. They could be rewarded with a sticker or have their name put on a 'Best player' list. Children could be asked to nominate each other.

The choice of activity will depend on the space available and the mood of the children. This book is divided into the following chapters:

Chapter 1: Circle games

These are sociable games that make good icebreakers and encourage all children to participate. The children sit or stand in a circle to play, so these games are suitable for a hall or a classroom where the desks can be moved back. If there is a reasonable area at the front of the class, smaller groups of children could take turns to play a circle game while others enjoy games from the other chapters.

To get children to form a circle, ask them to join hands, then let go and step back if necessary (they can touch fingers or hold wrists if they do not want to hold hands).

Chapter 2: From the front
These games are led from the front of the class by an adult play leader. They are suitable for engaging children's attention and controlling a large group within a classroom environment.

The children and the play leader will have their own ideas for items and topics, but the games are faster and smoother if there are plenty of ideas to back these up. The photocopiable pages at the end of the chapter will help here.

Children who do not wish to stand in front of the class may feel more comfortable standing in their own place.

Chapter 3: Table buddies
These activities and games are suitable for small groups of children to do together at the same table. They allow the children to get on with the game while the teacher or classroom assistant concentrates on their own work.

Each table can play a different game at the same time. Prepare a lucky game dip by photocopying different activity pages, one for each table, folding them and putting them into a container. It is best to choose activities that do not need equipment for this. Choose a child from each table to pick one. This way they have the instructions on hand to refer to as they play. Children from each table can play for a set amount of time before swapping their photocopies of the activity with the next table so they can try a different game.

It is a good idea to appoint a play leader for each table whether the games need one or not, so that they can deal with disputes, ensure that things run smoothly and that everything is tidied up at the end of the session.

Chapter 4: Twos and threes
These games and activities are ideal for children who are sitting in pairs, and are also useful when the play leader wishes to break large table groups into smaller groups. The games are mostly designed for two children, but easily adapt to be played in threes. They are also useful for occasional moments of free time, for instance while lining up or waiting for the teacher.

Chapter 5: Physical fun
Here are a choice of physical games and challenges that can be enjoyed in a furniture-free area in a classroom or a school hall. The games are good for children who have had wet play all day, are getting restless and need to let off steam. Some of these games can be adapted for a more confined area so that children can get some physical action, whatever the weather.

In an area that is not normally used for physical games, it is important to do a risk assessment first. The children can help by looking out for anything that could be dangerous. For example, things that they could trip over or sharp edges they could fall against. These can be dealt with by moving or covering them, or creating an inner boundary to play in.

Chapter 6: Paper capers
These simple craft activities can be done with little supervision, although younger children may need help with cutting. Photocopiable sheets that need to be copied onto card could be photocopied onto paper and stuck onto cheap card (for example, cereal packets).

CHAPTER 1

Circle games

AGE RANGE 5–11

SUMMARY
An easy game to learn and a good icebreaker.

Zombies

What you need
A large, clear space.

What to do
● The children stand in as wide a circle as space allows.
● Matt is chosen to be the 'zombie'. He stands in the middle.
● When the game begins, he walks with his arms outstretched towards another child in the circle. He chooses Jenny.
● To divert him, Jenny has to say somebody else's name before he reaches her. Jenny says *Luke* and the zombie turns and heads towards Luke.
● Luke then has to call out someone else's name before Matt reaches him.
● If Jenny does not speak in time, zombie Matt puts his hands on her shoulders and she becomes the zombie.
● If someone wrongly assumes that Matt is coming towards them and calls out a name then they sit out of the game until there is a new zombie.
● The game can be played with the same zombie and children who are caught going out of the game so that the circle gradually shrinks. As it gets smaller the zombie should get faster and faster.

Ground rules
Explain that it is not worth stepping backwards to avoid the zombie, because anyone who does so is considered caught and becomes the zombie.

Differentiation
The game can be played with the zombie moving slowly or quickly depending on the age and ability of the children. The zombie can change speed to confuse the children, or for large groups of older children the game can be played with two zombies.

Another variation is for the children in the circle to call out specific criteria, for example *Black hair* or *Wearing a watch*. The zombie walks towards anybody who fulfils this criterion. However, the children in the circle must choose their criterion by looking to ensure that it exists within their circle, or they will be out.

A very fast version is for the children to pass round an object behind their backs. The zombie races around putting his hand on children's shoulders. They respond by putting their hands on his, or by giving him the object if they have it. He then chooses the next zombie.

AGE RANGE 5–11

SUMMARY
This game gets everybody giggling.

If you're happy

What you need
Chairs arranged in a circle (if the children do not want to sit on the floor).

What to do
● Children sit in chairs or on the floor in a circle.
● Kadie is 'It'. She goes into the middle of the circle and has to pick someone. She kneels in front of Haris and says *If you're happy Haris, just smile.*
● Haris answers *I am happy Kadie, but I just can't smile.* If he does smile or laugh then it is his turn to be 'It'. If not, Kadie has to try to make somebody else laugh.
● The game can be played with no words. The child in the centre kneels in front of someone and pulls a funny face and the other child has to copy it without laughing. Alternatively, the child in the centre should very gently touch the nose of the child that they are kneeling in front of. This child must reciprocate while keeping a straight face.

Ground rules
● The child who is 'It' can make a funny face, change their voice, smile and laugh, but they cannot touch the child they are speaking to, unless they are playing the final variation where they touch each other's noses.
● Everybody else can laugh, but the child who is 'It' is the only one who should deliberately make somebody else laugh. However, you could decide that nobody is allowed to laugh and if anybody does they have to pay a forfeit or be excluded from the game.

Differentiation
Younger children can play the game 'Boo' because the words are easier to remember. The game is the same, but Kadie says *Boo!* and Haris answers *Boo to you too.* Older groups can say *Boo* and answer *You can say Boo, but you can't scare me.* Encourage children to think of other variations for this game, either funnier things to say or silly actions to do. Sometimes the simplest actions can seem hilarious when everybody is trying not to laugh.

Wet Playtimes **BRIGHT IDEAS**

AGE RANGE 5–8

SUMMARY
This is a quiet game, good for calming children down ready for lessons.

Who has the keys?

What you need
A blindfold; a bunch of keys or a bell.

What to do
● Children sit on the floor in a circle for this game.
● Jamila is 'It'. She is blindfolded and sits in the middle of the circle.
● A bunch of keys or a bell is placed in front of her.
● Choose someone sitting in the circle to remove the keys.
● Bianca creeps up to Jamila and takes the keys as silently as possible. Then she returns to her place and holds them behind her back.
● All the other children put their hands behind their backs.
● Ask Jamila to take off the blindfold.
● Jamila can ask the children up to five questions before she makes her guess who has the keys. The other children can only answer *Yes* or *No* by nodding or shaking their heads. So Jamila might ask *Does a girl have the keys?* or *Does a blond-haired boy have the keys?*
● After her questions Jamila has three guesses as to who has the keys. If she guesses correctly she can choose who is to be blindfolded next. If not, the child with the keys is blindfolded for the next game.

Ground rules
● Explain that everyone must be quiet to help the child in the middle hear the keys being removed and where they are taken.
● Suggest that, to add confusion, the child taking the keys walks around the circle before going to their place.
● If the child in the middle hears the keys being removed, they can try to touch the child who is taking them. If they succeed, somebody else is chosen to take the keys. If they miss, the child who was trying to take the keys takes their place.

Differentiation
Some children do not like wearing blindfolds, so they could close and cover their eyes and promise not to peep! Shy children can play the game without having to go in the middle of the circle.

AGE RANGE 5–11

SUMMARY
A fast-moving game that allows children to let off steam in small areas.

Whacker

What you need
Chairs arranged in a circle; a rolled-up newspaper (the 'whacker'); a box or hoop.

What to do
● Children sit on chairs arranged in a circle. The box or hoop is placed in the middle.
● Charlie is 'It' and does not have a chair. He stands in the middle holding the rolled-up newspaper – the 'whacker'.
● He walks around with the whacker. The children do not know who he is going to tap, but they must be ready to move fast. Charlie taps Asja on the leg, puts the whacker in the box or hoop and tries to sit in her chair. Asja leaps up, picks up the whacker and tries to tap him back before he sits down.
● If she taps him before he sits down, he keeps the whacker and tries again with somebody else.
● If he sits down before she taps him, then Asja is 'It'.

Ground rules
● The whacker should be made from just a few sheets of newspaper, so that it does not hurt anybody.
● Explain that the children must tap and not whack the newspaper down. If they hurt anybody it will spoil the game for everybody.
● The children must only tap the other players below the waist. If they tap anyone above the waist then they must sit out of the game for the next round, and if they do this more than once they must be excluded permanently.

Differentiation
Older children will enjoy bluffing by pretending they are going to tap somebody and then tapping somebody else. Young children who are 'It' can have an (empty) chair of their own so that they have a choice of two to flee to.

Wet
Playtimes BRIGHT IDEAS

AGE RANGE 5–11

SUMMARY
Observation, action and fast response make this a popular indoor game.

Wink rescue

What you need
Chairs arranged in a circle (enough for half the group plus one extra).

What to do
● Half the children sit on chairs in a circle and the others stand behind them, one behind each chair.
● One child must be standing behind an empty chair. If the number of children is even, so that nobody is left behind the empty chair, choose two children to each stand behind an empty chair.
● Kim is standing behind the empty chair. She winks at Lucy who is sitting on a chair in front of Angelo.
● Lucy sees her wink and has to run to the empty chair in front of Kim, before Angelo realises that she is escaping. If he does, he puts his hands onto her shoulders to stop her. He is too late and Lucy escapes to Kim's chair.
● Now it is Angelo's turn to wink at somebody to try to get them to fill his (now) empty chair. He winks at Claire who is sitting in front of Rob. Claire runs to sit in front of Angelo and it is Rob's turn to wink at somebody to get them to sit in his chair.
● If there are two children behind two empty chairs, they each take turns to wink. For example, Kim and Jon are behind the empty chairs. Kim winks at Lucy who leaves Angelo and sits in front of her. It is now Jon's turn to wink.
● Halfway through the game, the children who are sitting swap places with those who are standing. The child or children behind the empty chairs will need to swap with somebody who does not want to sit down. Otherwise, they should remain standing and swap with somebody after further play.

Ground rules
Children standing behind the chairs must have their hands by their sides and only put them onto their captives' shoulders to stop them escaping. The captives must then remain in the chair. This will ensure there is no clothes pulling or rough play.

Differentiation
Young children may have to blink and nod, because winking may be difficult for them.

AGE RANGE 5–8

SUMMARY
A crazy game with no purpose or outcome, just lots of fun and laughter!

Pile up

What you need
Chairs arranged in a circle (enough for one per child).

What to do
- All the children sit on chairs.
- Choose a play leader to ask the children to move around the circle of chairs in a clockwise or anticlockwise direction, according to specific criteria. Children really enjoy being the play leader for this game.
- Clare is the play leader. She asks children who are wearing blue socks to move two spaces clockwise.
- Timmy, Pria and Daisy move two spaces. All the chairs have other children sitting on them, so they sit on their laps.
- Then Clare asks children with brown eyes to move five spaces anticlockwise.
- Guy, Anoushka, John, Gina, Farzhad, Pria and Timmy move round. Now some chairs have three children sitting on top of each other and everybody is giggling.
- To bring the game to an untidy end, the play leader can deliberately choose moves that get the children sitting in piles of three or four.
- The same game can be played with children racing back to their own seats. They put a sticker or Post-it Note where they are sitting and the play leader can only choose moves in one direction. The first child to go all the way round back to their seat is the winner.

Ground rules
- Remind the children to sit on each other's laps gently. Keep an eye on pile ups to ensure that the bottom child is happy.
- Children can leave the game instead of sitting on somebody's lap. They then help the play leader choose the next criteria, direction and number of moves.
- If a child is the play leader, keep a close eye on how the game progresses for safety reasons.

Differentiation
Some children will need the play leader to show them which way round to move. Children up to the age of 11 enjoy playing this game if they are in a group with their friends.

AGE RANGE 8–11

SUMMARY
An unusual and popular game with one clear winner.

Catchfingers

What you need
A large, clear space.

What to do
● Choose a play leader. The rest of the children stand in a circle.
● The play leader calls *Number one*, and all the children hold out their right hands, open-palmed and up to the level of their shoulder.
● The play leader calls *Number two*, and all the children put their left forefinger and middle finger flat on the palm of their neighbour's hand.
● When the play leader calls out *Number three*, the children have to try to grip the fingers of the child on their right, while trying to save their own from getting caught by the child on their left.

● Children whose fingers are caught have to step away and the remaining players form a smaller circle. The game continues until there are two remaining players who stand opposite each other for the Catchfingers final.

Ground rules
● Children can have some trial runs to get the hang of the game before the elimination starts.
● Show the difference between catching by closing your hand sharply, and by yanking, pulling or being rough. Children who are rough will not be able to play.
● If there is a dispute as to whether fingers have been caught and the play leader did not see what happened, they can allow a two-player challenge. This is played with the two disputing players only, as in the Catchfingers final. If Mark disputed that his finger was caught by Chloe in the main game they could have a challenge. If Mark is caught by her in the challenge he must sit out. If he catches Chloe's fingers in the challenge, they both return to the game.

Differentiation
Try this game with small groups of younger children, but use the words *flat hands*, *pointy fingers* and *catchfingers* instead of using counting instructions. Show the children what each of these instructions mean. Play the game without eliminating children who get their fingers caught.

AGE RANGE 5-8

SUMMARY
Good observation and bluff are the main features of this game.

Who started it?

What you need
A large, clear space.

What to do
● Children can play this standing, sitting on chairs or on the floor.
● Laine is chosen to be 'It' and turns away, or waits outside the door.
● Polly is chosen as action leader and has to perform a series of actions for the others to copy.
● Polly claps her hands, then rubs her head. She stamps her feet and nods her head. She keeps changing her actions and the other children copy her as she moves, while continuously changing her actions.
● Laine is called and returns to watch. The children continue to copy Polly, and Laine tries to see who they are all copying.
● Laine has to guess who the leader is. She can have five guesses. If she guesses correctly she chooses who is going to be 'It' in the next game. If not, Polly can choose.

Ground rules
● Explain that it is important not to stare at the action leader as it will give the game away. The children should copy by using their peripheral vision and glancing at the action leader once in a while.
● Encourage the children to bluff by staring at other children, so that 'It' might think that someone else is the action leader.
● In smaller groups 'It' should have three guesses instead of five, and if there are less than eight children then only one guess is allowed.

Differentiation
Older children can play a variation of the game where the action leader moves in exaggerated slow motion, or in the manner of a favourite soap or pop star. There is usually much hilarity as everyone synchronises their movements while trying not to giggle at the action leader's portrayal of the chosen character.

   Another variation is for the action leader to perform one action and then to stop and sit with feet together and hands in their laps. They then perform another action and then stop, so that instead of continuous actions there are pauses in between, giving 'It' more of a chance to spot who starts the action.

AGE RANGE 5–11

SUMMARY
This game is not as easy as children think it is going to be!

Handy ID

What you need
A large, clear space.

What to do
- All the children stand in a circle.
- Siu Mei is chosen to be in the middle.
- She points at Cassie with her right hand and says *Who's next?*
- Cassie has to say the name of the child on her right – *Conrad*.
- If Siu Mei had pointed with her left hand, Cassie would have said the name of the child on her left – *Jade*.
- Siu Mei continues to ask different children *Who's next?* while pointing with her right or left hand.
- This game can be played with the child who is 'next' stepping forward. For example, Siu Mei points to Cassie with her right hand and asks *Who's next* and Conrad steps forward and says *I'm next*. If she pointed to Cassie with her left hand then Jade would step forward and say *I'm next*.
- Children take turns to go in the middle.

Ground rules
- If the child being asked *Who's next* hesitates, they are out and must sit down.
- The children should remember that if Siu Mei is facing them, her left-hand side is their right-hand side, and vice versa.
- Other children, especially those on either side of the child being asked the question, are not allowed to hint or help by nudging the child that is being asked.
- If the game is being played where the child who is 'next' should respond, if they do not step forward immediately they are out.

Differentiation
This game sets its own pace. Younger children will take their time to ask *Who's next?* and children in the circle will need longer to respond. Older children are much faster. To make it even more difficult, older children can swap places frequently throughout the game.

Another variation is for the child in the middle of the circle to point to somebody and ask questions such as *Who's tall?*, *Who's black-haired?*, *Whose name begins with 'B'?* The child they are pointing to has to point to a child that fulfils the criteria.

AGE RANGE 5–11

SUMMARY
A game that encourages teamwork and gets children giggling.

Scrambulation

What you need
A large, clear space.

What to do
● All the children stand in a circle.
● Sasha is the 'unscrambler'. She stands outside the circle of children.
● The children put their right hands out and take somebody else's hand. Then they do the same with their left hands.
● They must stay linked in this 'scrambulation' while Sasha tries to unscramble them by telling them where to move and what to do until they are all in a circle again.
● The time Sasha takes to unscramble them is written on a score sheet so children can compete to see who can do it in the quickest time.
● Alternatively, the unscrambler can be given a time limit. If they have not managed to unscramble the children in the given time, another unscrambler is chosen and children start the game again.

Ground rules
● Children must keep hold of each other's hands until they have been unscrambled or time has run out.
● The unscrambler must not touch the other children, they can only give directions.
● Children must follow the directions of the unscrambler and must not try to unscramble themselves.
● It does not matter if the children are facing in or out of the final circle.
● Supervise the game closely for safety reasons.

Differentiation
Younger unscramblers may need some guidance from the play leader. Young children often break hands while doing complicated moves and tend to rejoin them in an easier position. Play leaders can turn a blind eye!

An alternative is for children to start by holding hands in a circle. Then the unscrambler turns their back and counts to 20, while the children make themselves into a scrambulation by climbing over or going under each other's arms – they must keep hold of each other's hands for this. The unscrambler has to try to unscramble the children to the count of 20.

CHAPTER 2

From the front

AGE RANGE 5–11

SUMMARY
A simple game that is easy for children of all abilities to play.

Alteration

What you need
No equipment required.

What to do
● The aim of the game is to see if the children can spot something that another child has altered about their appearance.
● The play leader chooses two children to go to the front to start this game.
● Akbar and Joey are chosen to go to the front. They turn around slowly so that the children in the class can take a good look at them.
● Afterwards, they go outside the classroom and change something about the way they look. Akbar puts his watch on the other wrist and Joey puts his shoes on the wrong feet.
● When they return Akbar and Joey turn around slowly so that the other children can have another look to see if they notice the changes that have been made to their appearances.
● If the children are finding it hard to guess the changes that have been made, they can ask questions which Akbar and Joey must answer *Yes* or *No* to. For example, Sarah asks *Is the change on your legs or feet?* Joey answers *Yes*, but Akbar answers *No*.
● The children who are first to spot the alterations in appearance have the next turn at the front.

Ground rules
● The alteration must show and be specific. For example, changing socks that are hidden by long trousers or jewellery worn under long sleeves is not acceptable.
● The play leader should advise on the alterations where necessary.

Differentiation
Explain the types of changes that might be made so that younger or less able children know what to look for. Young children or children with learning disabilities who are making alterations may need help with ideas from the play leader. Children with physical disabilities may need help to alter their appearance.

AGE RANGE 7–11

SUMMARY
Fast talking and a good imagination are needed for this game.

Gift of the gab

What you need
A bag full of randomly chosen items from the classroom for children to 'sell'; a flipchart and writing materials.

What to do
● The aim of the game is for a child to try to sell a randomly selected object to the rest of the class, and to find out if they have the 'gift of the gab'.
● Kelly is chosen to be the first 'salesperson' and goes to the front.
● The play leader offers her the bag containing random items from the classroom. Kelly puts her hand in without looking and pulls out a marble.
● Kelly has to talk about the marble for 30 seconds, as though she were trying to sell it. She should tell the other children all the great things about the marble, what they can do with it and alternative uses for it. For example, she might suggest that it would be a good football for a hamster, or a paperweight for small notes.
● After this, all the children who would buy it on the basis of her sales pitch stand up, and those who would not remain seated.
● The number of 'buyers', as represented by the number of children standing, is written next to Kelly's name on a large score sheet.
● Then the play leader chooses somebody else to be the salesperson.

Ground rules
● If the salesperson is struggling for ideas, they can call *Help* and choose a friend to join them at the front to help them sell their item.
● Encourage the children to vote on the basis of the sales pitch rather than who their friends are.

Differentiation
Depending on the age and ability of the children, the time limit can be extended to one minute or reduced to 15 seconds. This has the effect of slowing down or speeding up the game. It is hard to talk for one minute on a single object, but equally hard to sell it in ten seconds!

AGE RANGE 7–11

SUMMARY
Budding actors and actresses really enjoy this game.

Answer me... grumpily

What you need
Copies of the 'Answer me... grumpily' photocopiable sheet on page 27 (one for the play leader and one for each table).

What to do
● The play leader should explain that in this game 'It' should ask open questions, so that children have to answer more than *Yes* or *No*. For example, *What do you like about school?* rather than *Do you like school?*

● Deanna is 'It' and stands outside the classroom. Using ideas from the photocopiable sheet (or ideas of their own, the children suggest an adverb.
● The play leader chooses Joey's suggestion, which is 'shyly'.
● Deanna returns and asks individual children questions. She can ask the same question to lots of different children, or lots of questions to the same or different children.
● All children answer her as though they were shy.
● Deanna has to try to guess that they are answering shyly.
● Deanna can ask ten questions. After this she has three guesses to see if she knows the adverb.
● If she guesses correctly she can choose the adverb for the next game.
● If she is wrong she can ask five more questions. This time children must really exaggerate their response to help her to guess. She can have three more guesses before the play leader tells her what the adverb was.
● Then someone else is chosen to be 'It' and the group can choose another adverb.

Ground rules
Children who do not feel they can respond in a certain way can pass when asked a question and somebody else can be asked the question instead.

Differentiation
The adverbs on the photocopiable sheet are listed as easy, harder and hardest, which will help younger and older children, and those of varying abilities. Choose the most appropriate.

The play leader should be prepared to demonstrate how to respond, especially with younger children.

AGE RANGE 7–11

SUMMARY
There are some very funny results with this game.

Loony limericks

What you need
A whiteboard or flipchart and writing materials; copies of 'Loony limericks' photocopiable sheet on page 28; pens/pencils; paper.

What to do
● Each group or table of children is given a copy of the 'Loony limericks' photocopiable sheet. The children read a few limericks out loud to get used to the rhythm and rhyming patterns.
● Shane is chosen to make up the first line of a limerick and to write it on the board.
● Children have a few minutes to think of the next line, and then the play leader chooses Ann to write hers underneath Shane's.
● George is chosen to write the third line, and Vicky the fourth.
● The class should think of a funny last line. The play leader can listen to a few suggestions and choose the funniest. That child gets to complete the limerick on the board.
● The class and the play leader say the limerick together and those who wish to have a few minutes to copy it.
● Then another child is chosen to write the first line of another limerick and the game continues.
● The play leader could suggest a theme or word endings to see how many rhymes the children can think of. If these are written on the board it will help children to think of lines for their limericks.

Ground rules
● Suggest possible alterations to the last word on the first and third lines, to ensure that there are plenty of rhyming words.
● Children may share and discuss ideas together in their groups, but must be quiet when the play leader asks to allow the game to continue.

Differentiation
Children from the age of five can play this game with extra guidance from the play leader. They can think of ideas for each line, but the play leader may need to help with the rhythm and rhyme and in writing the words on the board.

    After a couple of rounds of this game, older children can make up limericks at their tables and then read them out to the rest of the class.

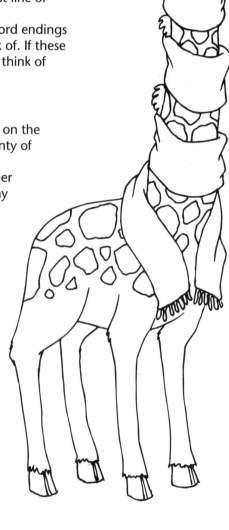

AGE RANGE 7–11

SUMMARY
Bingo, especially tailored for school playtimes.

Board bingo

What you need

Copies of the 'Board bingo – game board' photocopiable sheet on page 29 (enough for the play leader for each game played) and of the 'Board Bingo – play sheets' photocopiable sheet on page 30 (enough for each child in the class); pens or pencils; a whiteboard or flipchart and writing materials.

What to do

● The children are each given a copy of the 'Board bingo – play sheets' photocopiable sheet. They choose numbers between 1 and 50 and put a number in each of the empty squares in the 'Game 1' table.
● The play leader calls out a number between 1 and 50 and puts a cross on the corresponding number on their 'Board bingo – game board' photocopiable sheet. They write the number on the board so that the children can see it.
● Children with the same number in a square on their sheet put a cross on that square, making sure that the number is still clearly visible.
● Alex is the first to get four crosses in a row. He shouts *Bingo* and receives five points.
● Laura is the first to cross out all 16 squares on her sheet. She shouts *Full house* and gets 10 points.

Ground rules

● Every number that the children write down in a table should be different.
● Children must not copy each other.
● When children have finished writing their numbers, ask them to hold them up for you to see. This makes sure that nobody writes their numbers as they are being called – it has been known!
● 'Bingo' can be called for numbers in a row, a column or in a diagonal line.
● The play leader checks the winning children's numbers before awarding points.

Differentiation

The game can be simplified by using numbers 1 to 25 for the game and asking children to fill in the first eight squares with these numbers. 'Bingo' is called for four in a horizontal row, and 'Full house' when all eight squares are crossed off.

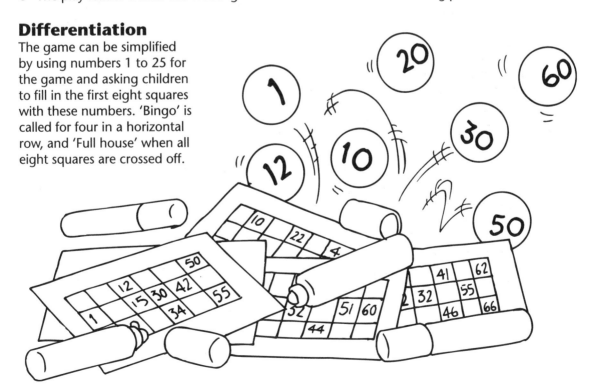

AGE RANGE 5–11

SUMMARY
Acting, improvisation and
entertainment keeps everybody
happy.

Silly sketches

What you need
Copies of 'Silly sketches' photocopiable sheet on page 31
(enough for groups of three), cut along the dotted
lines; a container to hold the slips of paper.

What to do
● The play leader puts all the slips of
paper cut from the photocopiable
page into a container.
● The play leader asks all the
children who wish to act in a
sketch to get into groups of two
or three. They invite each group
to take three slips of paper from
the container.
● The children have a few
minutes to prepare their sketches,
which should include each word
on their slips of paper. Those who
don't want to act can help with ideas
for the sketch.
● Candice and Denzil are chosen first.
They had the words 'jelly', 'accident' and
'aeroplane', and make up a sketch about
a woman who makes a jelly in the shape of an
aeroplane and accidentally drops it on her son's lap.
● Next, Lucy and Meena do their sketch, which includes the words 'London', 'India'
and 'toothbrush'. In their sketch they travel from London to India for a holiday, but
Meena insists on returning to London because she forgot to pack her toothbrush.
● The other groups can enjoy the sketch and try to guess the significant words.

Ground rules
● The sketches must include each word on the slips of paper.
● All groups who wish to act should pick their slips of paper and prepare their sketches
at once. This way everybody can be involved at the same time, either by acting or
helping with ideas. Otherwise, children will be restless while waiting for each group to
prepare.
● When watching the sketches everybody agrees to be quiet and listen.

Differentiation
Young children can improvise a sketch using just one or two words.

AGE RANGE 8–11

SUMMARY
A clever game leading to some very strange conversations.

What's the plot?

What you need
A whiteboard and writing materials.

What to do
● The aim of the game is to include a chosen subject in a conversation so that others can guess what the subject is.
● The play leader writes some subject suggestions on the board. For example, *sport, food, school, animals, weather, toys, families.* More difficult examples could include *items made of wood, seasons, hobbies, feelings.*
● The play leader asks for two volunteers. Carol and Farzhad are chosen. They sit facing each other in front of the class.
● The play leader lets them choose a subject from the list. Carol chooses 'food' and Farzhad opts for 'sport', but they have to keep their choices to themselves.
● Carol and Farzhad converse with each other. They must include their own subject each time they speak, but they have to disguise it as much as possible. The conversation might proceed as follows:
    Carol: 'Didn't I see you in the lunch queue today? It took ages, didn't it?'
    Farzhad: 'Yes, it took so long I would not have been able to play football, even if it had stopped raining.'
    Carol: 'I know. I'm glad they had treacle sponge and custard left after that long wait. It's my favourite.'
    Farzhad: 'I had some today, but I wouldn't eat any if I were playing sport afterwards.'
● As the conversation continues, the other children have to guess what the subjects are. Jenny guesses that Farzhad's subject is sport. She chooses another subject from the list and takes his place. Carol continues talking with Jenny about her subject 'food'.
● When Luke guesses that Carol's subject is food, he selects another from the list and takes her place.

Ground rules
● Explain that the children must put their hands up to guess the subjects, because calling out will prevent other children from hearing the conversation.
● Explain that the children do not have to use the specific word (for example, 'food' or 'sport'), but must discuss the topic. Carol mentioned 'lunch' and 'treacle sponge and custard', and Farzhad mentioned 'football' as well as 'sport'.

Differentiation
The play leader can select the subjects instead of allowing the children to choose.

AGE RANGE 5–11

SUMMARY
A fast, competitive game for table teams.

Superstore

What you need
A whiteboard or flipchart and writing materials.

What to do
● The class needs to be divided into groups of four to six for this game. This is easily done if they are already sitting at tables of this number.
● The play leader calls out an item which the groups might have at their tables at that moment. The items could include a watch, a calculator, a pencil sharpener, a hair scrunchie or band, a specific shape, coins, an item beginning with a specific letter of the alphabet. You could specify colours or details to make the game more of a challenge. For example, a patterned pencil case, a blue sock, two red pens, two ties tied together.
● The first child to stand, holding up the item, scores a point for their team.
● The team with the most points at either the end of playtime, a set time limit or 20 item requests, is the winner.

Ground rules
● Whoever has the item must stand and hold it up to win the point. Remind the children that this is a team game, so they should all be looking at the others on their table to see if any of them have the item that is asked for.
● Suggest that the children all have a good look at themselves, at each other and at what they have in their bags before the game starts, so that they are prepared when the play leader asks for an item.

Differentiation
To make the game harder, ask the teams to choose a representative to stand and hold up the item. This means that whoever has the item has to pass it to this child to hold up.

In a spacious classroom or hall, teams can either sit in groups around the edge with the play leader standing in the middle, or stand in groups along one wall while the play leader stands by the opposite wall. A child from each team can race to the play leader with the requested item.

AGE RANGE 5–11

SUMMARY
A game of suspense that is great fun to play.

Bang!

What you need
Paper; pens or pencils; a chair; a cushion.

What to do
● Place a chair with a cushion on it at the front of the class.
● Divide the class into two teams and appoint a team leader in each.
● The team leaders write the name of a member of the opposing team on a piece of paper.
● The leader of team A writes the name 'Carlos' on a piece of paper and shows his team without the other team seeing. He puts it under the cushion on the chair at the front of the class – the hot seat!
● Team B's leader must send three children in turn to sit on the hot seat.
● First he sends Alec. Alec walks up and sits in the seat. Then he returns to his team.
● Then Gail is sent to sit on the hot seat, but she returns safely to her seat.
● Finally, the team leader sends Carlos. The opposing team (who know his name is under the cushion) shout *Bang!* as he sits down on the hot seat.
● Carlos is out and team B is down by one member.
● Now it is team B's turn to put the name of a child in team A under the cushion on the hot seat.
● The teams take turns to try to eliminate members of the opposing team.
● The winning team is the one with the most players at the end of the game.

Ground rules
Encourage the children to try to be quiet, so that when a team shouts *Bang!* everybody jumps.

Differentiation
Table teams can be paired off to oppose each other, so that two or three games can be taking place simultaneously.

AGE RANGE 5–11

SUMMARY
A game that gets children to think laterally and creatively.

Oojamaflip

What you need
A bag full of randomly chosen items; a whiteboard or flipchart and writing materials.

What to do
● The children play in table teams (exact numbers don't matter).
● The play leader pulls an item from the bag and asks *What's this oojamaflip?*
● The play leader goes round the classroom and asks each team in turn to give a possible use for the item, except its real purpose or name. So a paper clip might be an earring or a clothes fastener, and a lever arch file could be a ramp for a toy car.
● Teams who cannot think of anything on their turn are eliminated until one team remains.
● A team is eliminated if a member of the team calls out the object's real name or purpose.
● The last team remaining is awarded 10 points and the game starts again with the next object.

Ground rules
The play leader must decide whether a possible use for an object is acceptable. Ideas can be lateral and creative, but must be feasible (creatively speaking!). If clarification is needed, the play leader can ask the team to explain further.

Differentiation
Show the item to groups of younger children and allow them a few minutes to discuss ideas before the round starts. They should also be allowed longer to respond, whereas older groups should be ready on their turn!

Answer me... grumpily

EASY	HARDER	HARDEST
Sadly	Thoughtfully	Hysterically
Happily	Dreamily	Disdainfully
Cheekily	Jokingly	Hilariously
Shyly	Lovingly	Poetically
Grumpily	Irritably	Questioningly
Bossily	Vaguely	Flirtatiously
Sulkily	Teasingly	Dramatically
Sleepily	Worriedly	Cleverly
Foolishly	Childishly	Vociferously
Excitedly	Urgently	Defensively
Argumentatively	Guiltily	Fussily
Proudly	Hypnotically	Wildly
Impatiently	Pompously	Positively
Hungrily	Romantically	Fearfully
Nervously	Confidentially	Exactly

SCHOLASTIC

Loony limericks

There was once a rich aristocrat
Who started to get very fat
He learnt to skip
To juggle and flip
And became an acrobat.

There was a young boy from Poole
Who would not go to school
He watched telly all day
Then he went out to play
And he thought he was cool, the fool.

There was a solemn giraffe
Who was given a very long scarf
When it had been tied
His smile opened wide
And he started to laugh and laugh.

There was a little ant
Who said Boo to an elephant
The elephant started
And then she farted
And that was the end of the ant.

A lady who lived in a flat
Had a rather peculiar cat
It ate only baked beans
And we know what that means
Although she's too 'naice' to talk about that.

A lazy man called Ed
Spent all year in bed
When he tried to rise
He struggled in surprise
For his beard had become his bedspread.

© Deborah Sharpe

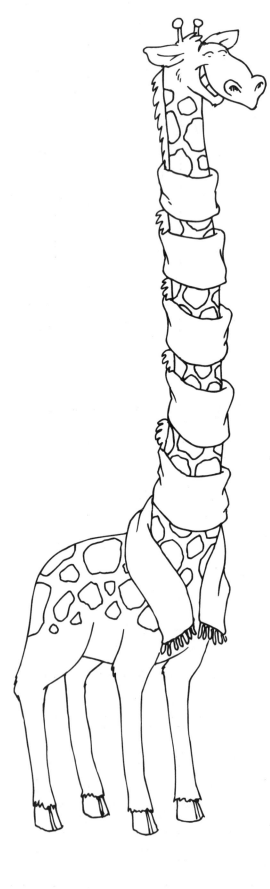

Wet Playtimes BRIGHT IDEAS

Board bingo – game board

1	2	3	4	5
6	7	8	9	10
11	12	13	14	15
16	17	18	19	20
21	22	23	24	25
26	27	28	29	30
31	32	33	34	35
36	37	38	39	40
41	42	43	44	45
46	47	48	49	50

Board bingo – play sheets

● Choose numbers between 1 and 50 and put one number in each box.

Game 1

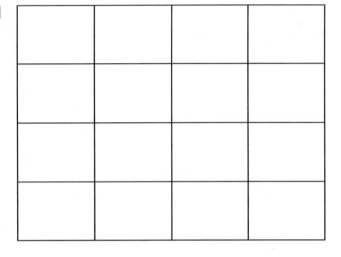

Game 2

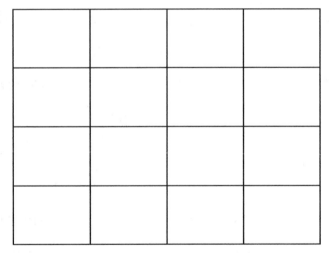

Game 3

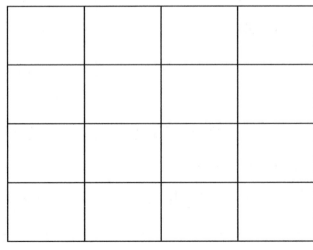

Silly sketches

● Cut out these words and see if you can include them in your 'silly sketches'!

India	Toothbrush	Meeting	Computer
Africa	Toast	Hug	Sports Day
Wales	Hat	Argument	Time
London	Trousers	Baby	School
Happy	Tree	Book	Hurry
Angry	Torch	Dad	Broom
Love	Dog	Mum	Accident
Crying	Elephant	Magic potion	Mirror
Hairstyle	Spider	Feather	Box
Excited	Run	Seaside	Gate
Lonely	Cook	Aeroplane	Tent
Climb	Jelly	Flowers	Bicycle

 Wet Playtimes

CHAPTER 3

Table buddies

AGE RANGE 5–11

SUMMARY
A popular creative activity that can be played as a card game.

Misfits

What you need
Copies of the 'Misfits' photocopiable sheet on page 42 copied onto card (enough for one per child or one between two); colouring pencils; scissors.

What to do
● Give each child the 'Misfits' photocopiable sheet and ask them to colour the characters. If they are sharing they should colour two characters each. Encourage the children to colour in the clothes with different patterns.
● Next, ask them to cut along the dotted lines so that the characters are in pieces – hats and heads, bodies, legs and feet.
● The children can experiment by putting different body part cards together to make 'misfits'. By swapping different cards with friends they will be able to make the most of

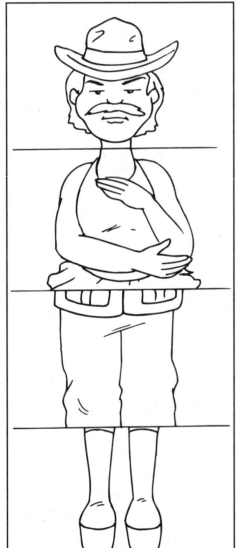

the different colours and patterns that they have used.
● For the Misfits game the children should work in small groups. All the cards should be muddled together and then laid face down individually on the table.
● The object of the game is to complete a misfit, working from the feet up or the head down.
● Each child takes a turn to pick a card. If it is a hat and head or feet they can keep it, if not they have to try again next time. On future turns, if they turn over another hat and head or feet before completing a character they can start another misfit and collect more than one misfit at a time.
● The game continues until all the cards have been collected. The child with the most completed misfits wins.

Ground rules
● Children should each take turns to select a card. They do not have an extra turn if they select a body part that they can keep.
● Children playing the Misfits game must start with a hat and head or pair of feet. Subsequent cards must complete the body from the hat down, or the feet upwards. For example, if Millie selects a pair of feet and then turns over a body, she cannot keep this because she needs a pair of legs first.

Differentiation
Children of all ages and abilities should find this easy, and even the cutting is in straight lines so only the youngest will need help with this.

AGE RANGE 8–11

SUMMARY
A clever game that needs good observation skills.

The passing game

What you need
A simple, single item (for example, a pencil, a book or a ruler).

What to do
● Carrie is chosen to be the leader. Take her aside from the rest of the group and explain that she is going to pass the object round the table, but has to choose certain criteria to qualify whether it is passed correctly. She may decide that both elbows should be on the table, or that it must be passed with the left hand only. She must decide this and tell you before she starts the game.
● Carrie passes a pencil to Harry, twisting and turning it in an elaborate sequence.
● Harry takes it and tries to pass it to Gina in the same way. Carrie says, *That is incorrect.*
● The children continue to try to pass the pencil correctly. Sometimes Carrie says, *That is correct* and sometimes she says, *That is incorrect.*
● The children try to discover why some moves are correct and others incorrect, when they all seem to be doing the same.
● Finally, Sam notices that every time Carrie

says that other children have passed the pencil correctly, they have their elbows on the table. When it is his turn, he starts to do this in an exaggerated way. Soon all the other children are copying him. When it has been passed correctly all the way round the table, it is Sam's turn to start passing the pencil using his own criteria.

Ground rules
● The real criteria must be obvious, and able to be seen or heard. So, for example, crossed feet under the table would not be allowed.
● The leader of each game can bluff as Carrie did, by twisting and turning the object or doing other things to stop the others noticing the real criteria.
● The child who guesses must exaggerate what he has seen so that all the children are clear that he has guessed and that it is his turn to be the leader of the next game.

Differentiation
This is quite hard for younger children to play without adult guidance. An adult could start them off with clear criteria, such as winking, nodding or passing with the left hand. Older children will bluff well, but must ensure that the rules are followed and their chosen criteria are not obscured by the bluff moves they do.

AGE RANGE 5–11

SUMMARY
Good coordination is needed for this wacky game.

Hand stomp stomp

What you need
No equipment required.

What to do
● Everybody puts their hands on the table and crosses them with their neighbour, so that each subsequent hand is somebody else's.
● Each hand must be slapped down on the table in the order that they are placed around it.
● If somebody slaps down twice, the movement changes direction and goes around the other way.
● If somebody slaps down when it is not their turn, or does not slap down when it is, they put the hand they used (or did not use and should have) behind their back.
● For example, Ciara, Jack, Maria and Lucien have a game. Ciara begins, and slaps her hand down on the table. Jack's hand is next so he slaps his. Maria is next, then Lucien. Then Ciara slaps down her other hand twice. So it is now Jack's turn again, then Maria and then Lucien. But Maria does not move because she does not realise it is her turn, so she puts the hand she should have slapped down behind her back. Lucien slaps down his other hand, then it is Ciara's turn again, and so on.
● Those that lose both hands are out of the game, and the remaining players move closer and cross hands to start again. Gradually players are eliminated until there are two remaining winners.

Ground rules
● The game sounds more complicated than it is. Allow children to play a few practice rounds without getting eliminated for errors.
● If a dispute takes place, the majority rule as to whether a child's hand is 'in' or 'out'.

Differentiation
Younger children can play without losing their hands or going out of the game. They should choose a play leader who helps them by pointing to the next hand that should be slapped down. If the play leader gets it wrong another is elected.

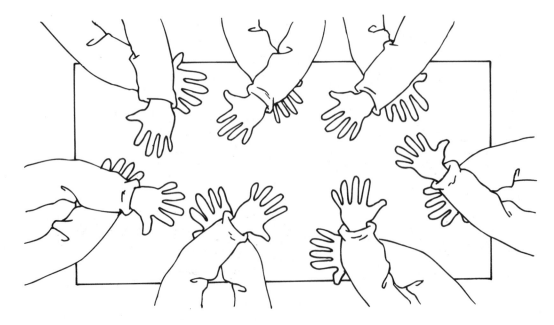

AGE RANGE 7–11

SUMMARY
Cutting and pasting newspaper headlines to create funny news stories.

Newspaper notices

What you need
Newspapers (about six for each table group); A3 paper (two or three sheets for each table group); glue sticks; scissors.

What to do
● Give each table group a selection of different types of newspapers. Let the children look through them and cut out interesting and amusing headlines and subheadings.
● Explain that, working together, the groups should arrange these onto their A3 paper to assemble a funny notice or report. They could assemble both a report and a notice if they are able.
● Explain that they can separate headlines or subheadings and join them to others, adding single words if necessary to make funnier sentences.
● Once they are happy with the results, tell them to stick their pieces of newsprint in place onto the A3 paper.
● Allow time for the children to read out their notice to each other at the end of the session. Examples might include:

The public has a right to stop the Prime Minister singing in the rain.
More rain is on the way.
Steps are being taken to minimize the damage.
Police reinforcements will be used if necessary.

Ground rules
Children must try to use sentences and word groups from headings and subheadings, rather than cutting out too many individual words or letters.

Differentiation
To make the game harder, give the children a theme – for example, a traffic report or a notice for the class. Less able or younger children could use pictures from comics, magazines or catalogues to make up a story.

AGE RANGE 5–11

SUMMARY
An old-fashioned game, which involves some dextrous manoeuvring and bluffing.

Up Jenkins

What you need
A coin.

What to do
● Grace is 'It' and stands away from the table.
● She turns away while the other children start passing a coin to each other under the table.
● The group call *Ready* and continue to pass the coin under the table. Grace turns around and watches them to try to see which children are passing the coin to each other.
● When she calls *Up Jenkins* all the children have to close their fists and raise their hands in the air.
● When she says *Down Jenkins* they put their palms down onto the table. Stuart, who has the coin, has to be careful not to let her hear it or let it show.
● Grace asks them to *Slide palms* and the children move their palms along the table.
● When she says *Fisticuffs* they form their hands into fists on the table.
● Grace tries to guess who has the coin.
● If her first guess is correct, she has another turn. If not, it is Stuart's turn to be 'It', because he had the coin.

Ground rules
● The child who is 'It' can ask the children to do 'fisticuffs' or 'slide palms' as many times as they wish before they guess who has the coin. All the children have to comply when asked to do this.
● Children are allowed to bluff and to pretend that they have the coin.

Differentiation
Use 10p or 2p coins for older children and 1p coins for children aged seven and under, whose hands are smaller.
   Two coins can be used so that there is more chance of 'It' guessing who has one. If 'It' guesses correctly, they choose somebody to be the next 'It' rather than having another turn. If not, somebody flips a coin for the children who had the coins to call heads or tails, and the winner is 'It' in the next game.

AGE RANGE 7–11

SUMMARY
A word game that is different every time.

Word rally

What you need
Copies of the 'Word rally' photocopiable sheet on page 43 (one per child, or one between two); pens or pencils; graph paper; rulers.

What to do
● Give the children the 'Word rally' photocopiable sheet. Explain that they have to complete the grid by finding words that relate to the column heading and that begin with the row letter. For example, a plant beginning with *M* is *Mint*.
● There are no set answers for the grid, but it will encourage the children to use their imagination and to develop their vocabulary. Explain that they can share ideas if they are stuck for words.
● When they have completed their grids, tell them that you want them to use the photocopiable sheet as a guide to create their own word rally grids.
● Explain that they will need to draw a grid with seven columns. The first column heading is left blank, but the children should decide on headings for the next six columns on the grid. Tell them they can choose any category. For example, sports, games, TV, films, bands, singers, towns, famous people, book titles, authors and so on.
● Then tell them to choose a word of six to ten letters and write it down the left-hand side – each letter in a box of its own.
● Ask the children to swap grids with children on another table. Then challenge them – the first to fill all the squares with words is the winner.

Ground rules
● The best words to choose to go down the left-hand side are those that do not have many repeated letters.
● If children cannot fill in all the squares, the winner is the one who has completed the most.
● Children in a table group should use the same word down the left-hand side. If they can't think of or agree on one, they should ask a play leader to decide.

Differentiation
Younger children should have smaller grids with words of six to eight letters down the left-hand side, and older children could choose words of eight to ten letters.

AGE RANGE 5–11

SUMMARY
Brilliant coordination, fast responses and teamwork make this game a hit.

The clap click game

What you need
No equipment required.

What to do

● The children need to move their chairs back from their tables so that they can clap and click their fingers.
● Every child around the table is numbered consecutively, starting with the leader, Paul, who is number one.
● Paul starts the rhythm, which is two claps and two clicks of his fingers.
● When everybody is following the rhythm in time, Paul calls his own number and another number in time to the clicks of his fingers.
● He does two claps, and then says *one* (in time to a click) and *four* (in time to a click).
● Jacky is number four, and she responds with clap, clap, *four, two* (in time to her clicks). Number two is Garth, who responds clap, clap *two, three* and so on.
● If anyone hesitates, loses the rhythm or calls the wrong number they take the place of the lowest number and everyone moves up. Hence, if Jacky, who is number four, misses her cue, she moves to take Geeta's place at number six. Geeta moves up to become number five, and Nadia moves from number five to become number four.
● The idea of the game is for children to work their way into the number one position.

Ground rules
The children cannot call the number of the child who just called theirs. So if Geeta calls *five, four*, Nadia, at number four, cannot respond *four, five*.

Differentiation
Children who cannot click their fingers can slap their hands down onto their legs instead. An easier version of the game is for the children to say their own and another child's name in time to the rhythm. Another is to play word association, saying the associated word on the last clap or slap down. For example, clap, clap, slap, *mouse*; clap, clap, slap, *cheese*; and so on.

AGE RANGE 5–11

SUMMARY
Children contribute a word at a time to make a crazy story.

One word stories

What you need
No equipment required.

What to do
● The simplest version of this game is for the children to say one word in turn as quickly as possible around the table to try to make up a story. So Callum might say *Once*, Josh *upon*, Nina *a* and Debbie *time*.

● To make it more difficult, the play leader can ask for the story to include certain items or topics, which can only be mentioned if saying them makes sense in the context of the story. For instance, if *dustbin*, *daisy* and *dolly* were the words, the one word story might proceed as follows:

Once – there – was – a – **dolly** – who – was – lost – and – nobody – could – find – her. – Her – owner – **Daisy** – looked – everywhere – and – all – her – friends – looked – too – but – nobody – could – find – her – because – she – was – in – the – **dustbin**.

● The game can also be played by prohibiting certain words, such as *and*, *who*, *because*, *be*, *once*, *only*, *was*, *could*, *they* and *said*. If somebody says a prohibited word the others must make a raspberry sound and the child who said it must think of another word.

● An even funnier game is to have a goal for the story that most of the children are trying to achieve, while one or two (depending on numbers playing) have to try to stop the story reaching the desired goal. For example, four children are trying to get the hero to visit a theme park, while two are trying to stop him getting there:

John – was – **not** – working – because – **he** – was – going – **away** – to – Chessington – **but** – luckily – he – **stopped** – and – went – **home.**

Ground rules
Children must say their word as quickly as possible, as hesitations will hold up the story and spoil the fun.

Differentiation
The simplest version of this game is suitable for young children, whereas older children will enjoy trying different variations.

The children can decide on items and topics to include in their story (or words to prohibit) by writing them on slips of paper, folding them and putting them into a container. Then they can pick these before each game.

AGE RANGE 5–11

SUMMARY
Children find out all kinds of things about each other in this simple game.

Factually

What you need
A copy of the 'Factually' photocopiable sheet on page 44 for each table group; paper; pencils.

What to do
● Choose a child in each group to write the other children's names down on a sheet of paper and ask them to keep score for this game.
● The children take turns to state a fact about themselves that they think will also apply to other children in the group. The suggestions on the photocopiable sheet will help here if they get stuck for ideas.
● Other children in the group raise their hands if the statement also applies to them, and are awarded a point each. The child who made the statement also gets a point.
● If the statement does not apply to anybody else then the child who made the statement does not get any points.
● Ellie says *I have a dog*. Charlie and Billy raise their hands, because they have dogs too. They get a point, and so does Ellie. Luke says, *My dad is a dentist*. Nobody raises their hand so Luke does not score a point.

Ground rules
● The statements must be positive. For example, the children cannot state *I do not have a cat*.
● Encourage the children to make truthful statements, and only to put their hands up if the statement applies to them.
● The children can challenge anyone at any time if they believe a statement does not apply to them. They are allowed to ask one question each to get to the truth. Then all the children, except the one being challenged, vote on whether they believe the statement applies to the child or not. The majority decide whether to award or withhold the point.
● Any child who is challenged and loses three times goes out of the game.

Differentiation
Younger children might prefer to play without keeping score.

AGE RANGE 5–11

SUMMARY
A nonsense game that puts
everyone in a good mood.

Po!

What you need
No equipment required.

What to do
● The children start the game seated.
● Kate starts by performing any action. She touches her nose.
● The next child, Sean, touches his nose and adds an action of his own. He claps once.
● Tina touches her nose, claps once and scratches her head.
● Lily touches her nose, claps once, scratches her head and sticks out her tongue.
● The children continue to do all the previous actions before adding one of their own, without smiling or laughing.
● If anybody smiles, laughs or gets the sequence wrong, they have to continue the game while standing. If they do so again, they are out.
● The winners are those that remain unsmiling while completing the correct sequence of actions. It rarely gets that far because everybody is usually laughing too much.
● This game can be played with noises and sounds of one or two syllables. For example, Kate says *Po*, Sean says *Po, Bubby*, Tina says *Po, Bubby, Haya*, and so on.

Ground rules
● All actions or sounds must be different.
● If everyone agrees in advance, the children can have an extra 'life' by standing up for the first error, putting their hands on their heads for the second and then going out on the third.

Differentiation
Allow younger children to play this game as a memory game, so that they can giggle and laugh. They are often better at remembering the sequence than older children, but worse at keeping a straight face!

Misfits

● Cut out these misfits. Colour them in and use them in your games.

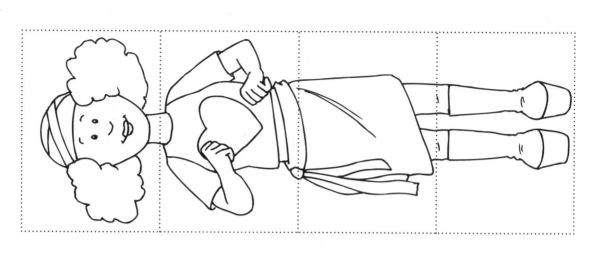

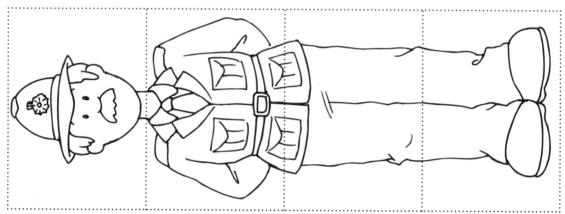

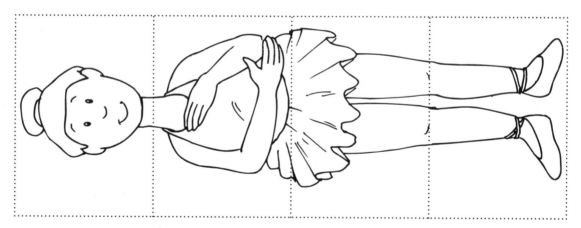

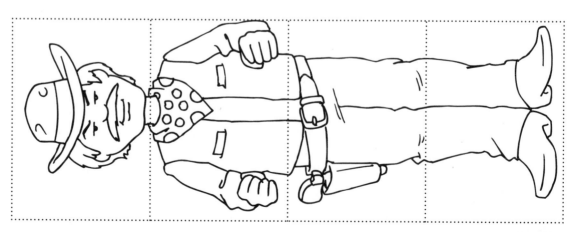

Wet Playtimes **BRIGHT IDEAS**

Word rally

● Complete this word rally. Some boxes have been completed for you.

	Animal	Building	Country	Plant	Food	Job
I						
M				Mint		
P						
O						
R						
T						Teacher
A						
N						
C	Cow					
E						

Factually

I have _____ **sister(s)/brother(s)**

My pet is a _____

I have _____ **pets** (state number)

My Mum/Dad's hair colour is

_____

My Mum is _____
(state job or profession)

My Dad is _____
(state job or profession)

My Mum/Dad goes to work by
☐ Bicycle
☐ Motorbike
☐ Car
☐ Train
☐ Bus

I live in a
☐ House
☐ Flat
☐ Bungalow
☐ Caravan

I travel to school
☐ On foot
☐ By bicycle
☐ By bus
☐ By train
☐ By car

I belong or go to
☐ Brownies or Cubs
☐ Horse riding
☐ A football club
☐ Another sports club
☐ Dance classes
☐ Music lessons
☐ Choir
☐ A drama club

I have been on holiday to

_____

I have visited _____
(state theme park or local attraction)

**I have been to the cinema to
see** _____

I watched _____
yesterday

I have read _____

My birthday is in _____
(state the month)

For my lunch I ate _____

_____

My coat/jacket is _____
(state colour)

My middle name begins with
_____ (state letter of the alphabet)

CHAPTER 4

Twos and threes

AGE RANGE 5–11

SUMMARY
Easy word games for two players.

Just words

What you need
Pencils; paper.

What to do
● **Guess who?**
Shane thinks of a person in the room and writes down their name, hiding it from Kelly. Kelly has twenty questions in which to find out who it is. Shane can only answer *Yes* or *No*. So Kelly cannot ask *Is it a girl or boy?* but has to ask *Is it a girl?*

● **Guess what?**
The children take turns in naming things for the other to spot. For example, Clare says *Spot something blue*, and Jonathon has to spot something blue as quickly as he can and say what it is. For example, *A blue box*.

Then it is Jonathon's turn. He says *Spot the word 'children'*. Clare sees it written on a poster on the wall and says *The poster says 'There are 12 children who walk to school'*.

● **The Yes, No game**
The children have to avoid saying *Yes* or *No* in response to the other's questions. Louise might say *Have you any pets?* and Patsy will answer *I have not*. Louise could say *Are you sure?* and Patsy would say *I am certain*. Whenever one of them says *Yes* or *No*, they swap roles.

● **Secret languages**
The children talk in a code language to each other. First they can practise putting 'ag' in front of the vowel sounds in words. So, *My name is Bianca* would become *Magy nagames Bagiagancaga*. After they have had fun with this, they can create their own secret language.

● **Animal chain-on**
The children think of animals that begin with the last letter of the previous one. For example, *cat, tiger, rabbit, toad, dog, giraffe, elk, kangaroo*.

● **The parson's cat**
The children take turns to think of attributes that the cat has beginning with 'A'. When someone cannot think of any more they move on to 'B'. For example, *The parson's cat is athletic, artistic, angry, African; beautiful, beige, bonny*. The child who said the last attribute beginning with 'A' gets a point.

Ground rules
● In the 'Yes, No' and 'Guess who?' games, the children cannot say 'yeah', nod or shake their heads, or say 'positive' or 'negative'. They can have a pre-determined number of questions to ask.
● In 'Guess what?' the other player can count to see how many seconds it takes before they see something that fulfils the criteria. They can try to beat each other's scores.

AGE RANGE 5–11

SUMMARY
Table football with minimal equipment.

Coin football

What you need
Two large coins and one smaller coin.

What to do
● Graham is the goalkeeper. He rests his open thumb and forefinger at the end of the table to make a V-shaped goal.
● Tamsin is the footballer. She starts on the edge of the table opposite Graham. She puts the two large coins about 10cm apart and a little way ahead of the small coin, which is the ball.
● Tamsin nudges the small coin through the gap between the other coins by pushing or flicking it with her forefinger.
● She then nudges one of the other coins through the gap made by the small coin and one of the other larger coins, aiming to leave another gap between two coins. A coin can only progress by going through the middle of the other two.
● Tamsin works the small coin down the table in this way, manipulating the coins so that when she is close enough to Graham's goal the small coin is in a good position for her to shoot.
● If she scores she gets 25 points for a goal, but has to deduct the number of coin nudges it took to get it (including shooting).
● Then she is the goalie and Graham is the footballer.
● If three children play, they take turns. The spectator can keep a tally of how many turns it takes the 'footballer' to score a goal.
● The winner is the player with the most points.

Ground rules
● The children are not allowed to put their fingers on top of the coins, but should push or flick them from the edge.
● Coins can only progress by going through the middle of the two others. They can move forwards or backwards.
● A player who has not left a gap large enough for another coin to pass through has to start again. If they score, 10 points are deducted, as well as the number of moves they made on their second turn. If it happens again they do not get another chance and it is somebody else's turn to be the footballer.

Differentiation
Allow everyone a few practice runs with the coins before the game starts.

AGE RANGE 5–11

SUMMARY
Children have to copy each other's pictures – without looking!

Mirror pictures

What you need
Plain paper; pencils; colouring pencils and pens.

What to do
● A large book is placed upright on the table between the two players, Akbar and Polly. Alternatively, they can turn their chairs round and sit back to back.
● They each draw a simple picture. This can be a specific item, like a house or car, or a pattern of shapes.
● Akbar describes his picture and Polly, following his instructions, tries to draw it onto a blank piece of paper.
● Then she describes her picture for him to draw.
● Finally, they compare pictures and see who has made the closest copy.
● If three children are playing, they should all draw pictures. Then each should take a turn describing their picture, while the other two try to draw an accurate copy.

Ground rules
● The children must describe the picture without saying what it is, or what part of the picture is. They can only describe shapes, lines, colours, and they can say where in the sheet the shapes should be. So they cannot say *Draw a face*, but would say *Draw a circle* and then go on to describe how to embellish it. For example, *Draw one small circle in the top-left quarter of the circle, one small circle in the top-right quarter of the circle and a curve in the bottom half of the circle.*
● If they are facing each other they are not allowed to draw shapes in the air to show what they mean.
● On each round, the children only see each other's pictures when they have copied one each.

Differentiation
Encourage older children to draw more complicated pictures or patterns, and to colour them in. This leads to more confusion and some very strange copies!

AGE RANGE 7–11

SUMMARY
A game of suspense that is also a good English exercise.

Letter by letter

What you need
Pencils or pens; paper.

What to do
● The children have to think of a word and take turns to write it out, a letter at a time. However, each will have a different word in mind. The player who completes a word first loses, so the children have to keep thinking of ways to extend the word without completing it.
● Deanna thinks of a word – *Castle* – and writes C on a sheet of paper.
● It is now Harry's turn. He decides on the word *Chair* and adds *h*.
● Deanna thinks of *Chocolate* and writes *o*, so Harry decides on *Choose* and adds another *o*.
● Deanna also thinks of *Choose* and writes *s* because she realises that now, Harry will have to complete the word.
● Harry cannot think of any other word that begins *choos* so he writes *e* and finishes the word *Choose*.
● Deanna gets the point.
● Three children can easily play this game by taking turns to add a letter.

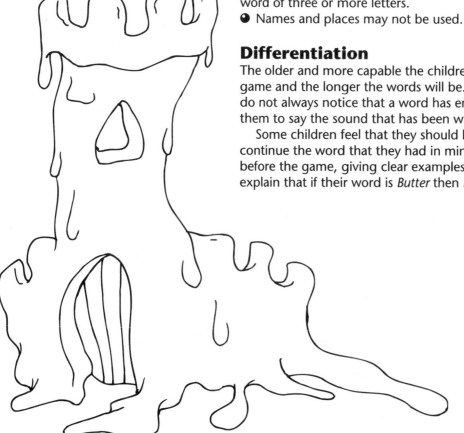

Ground rules
● The game stops when the letters make a complete word of three or more letters.
● Names and places may not be used.

Differentiation
The older and more capable the children, the harder the game and the longer the words will be. Younger children do not always notice that a word has ended, so encourage them to say the sound that has been written down.

Some children feel that they should be allowed to continue the word that they had in mind. Stress the rules before the game, giving clear examples. For instance, explain that if their word is *Butter* then *But* ends the game.

AGE RANGE 5–11

SUMMARY
A creative activity for the children to invent their own characters and settings.

Finger puppet soaps

What you need
Copies of the 'Finger puppet soaps' photocopiable sheet on page 55, copied onto card (enough for one between three children); scissors; glue sticks; sticky tape; felt-tipped pens or colouring pencils; A3 card or sugar paper.

What to do
● This is quite a long activity and needs a wet day where all the playtimes are likely to be indoors, or at least a lunchtime session.
● In groups of three, ask the children to think of an idea for a soap opera, or to choose a comedy or soap opera from television. They could also choose a favourite story or film.
● Give the groups a copy of the photocopiable sheet and ask the children to draw and colour in the characters that they need. Encourage them to draw in their own expressions, hairstyles, and so on. Suggest they add crowns, wizard hats or other accessories that they need.
● They can then cut out their characters and tape or glue them so that they can be worn as finger puppets.
● Then the children can decorate the A3 card or sugar paper to make it into a theatre. Show them how this can be folded in the centre so that it stands up on the table or the floor.
● Let the children practise putting their hands behind the theatre and popping their fingers up or down to bring on the characters.
● Ask the children to decide who will be the two actors and who will be the stage manager or director, who will decide on the story line and write down the lines for the actors to say.
● Let the children create scenes or sketches, or rehearse one that they have seen on television.
● Later, some could perform their scenes to the rest of the class.

Ground rules
● There are no limits unless the play leader wishes to ban certain television programmes from being used! Just encourage the children to use their imaginations and have fun.
● Encourage the children to use different voices for their characters.

Differentiation
Younger children will want to tell well-known stories or perform parts from favourite cartoon films. Older children love performing soap opera stories, popular cartoons and scenes from popular films like *Harry Potter* or *Lord of the Rings*.

AGE RANGE 5–11

SUMMARY
An easy and popular paper game that is a more interesting variation of noughts and crosses.

Paper four-in-a-row

What you need
Plain or squared paper; colouring pencils or felt-tipped pens.

What to do
● Ask the children to draw a grid of six-by-six squares on a sheet of paper. Explain that this means they will need seven horizontal lines and seven vertical lines, equally spaced.
● Playing in pairs, tell each child to have a different coloured pen to their partner. Explain that they should take it in turns to draw a circle, indicating a counter, in one of the squares on the grid, with the objective of getting four in a row.
● Explain that counters can only be drawn working from the bottom up, as though they are resting on each other. They cannot be drawn on top of empty squares.
● Tell the children that the first player to get four counters in a row, a column or diagonally is the winner.
● If three children are playing one will need to watch and play the winner in each round. Alternatively, children could draw lots to decide who plays each time.
● An alternative game is 'Squares', which also uses a grid of six-by-six squares. Using different coloured felt-tipped pens, players take turns to draw a line along one edge of one of the boxes on the grid.
● When a player completes a box they put their initials into it and have another turn.
● The player who has the most boxes at the end of the game wins.
● Three children can play at once, taking it in turns to draw a line along the edge of a box and counting who has the most boxes at the end.

Ground rules
● Remind the children to observe the other player's moves in 'Four in a row', so that they can block them and make it harder for their opponent to win.
● Whoever wins a game has the first turn on the next game.
● Suggest that players keep score of who wins the most games.

Differentiation
All age groups should find these games easy.

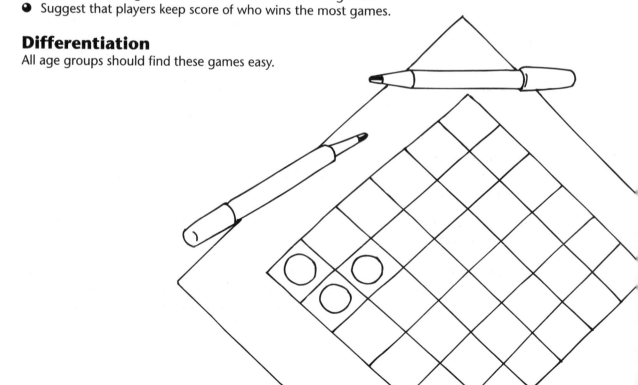

AGE RANGE 7–11

SUMMARY
Problems with some unusual solutions.

Silly sentences

What you need
Pens or pencils; A5 paper.

What to do
● Give a piece of paper to each child and ask them to fold the paper in half, and then unfold it again.
● Maria and Timothy write a problem on the top half of their piece of paper and fold the top over. Maria writes, *If my bike had a flat tyre…* on her piece of paper and Timothy writes, *If my cat was sick…* on his.
● They swap papers and write down the answer or solution to their problem on the other person's paper. So, for example, Maria writes, *I would pump it up again* on Timothy's paper, and Timothy writes, *I would take him to the vet.*
● Then they read them out. Maria and Timothy's papers would thus read, *If my bike had a flat tyre I would take him to the vet*, and *If my cat was sick I would pump it up again.*

● For a similar game – 'Silly story' – the paper needs to be folded into seven sections. The two players take it in turns to write the following sequence in each section (folding down the section after writing in it): a person or character, a second person or character, where the two met, something funny that happened, what the first person said, what the other replied and the outcome of the story.
● Then they can read out the story, using linking words to make the story flow. For example:

Harry met Minnie in the canteen and they accidentally bumped heads. Harry said, 'Can I have some sweets?' and she said, 'I like your hair', then they had a party and ate ice cream.

Ground rules
● Start off with a session where the children can suggest possible problems to give them all ideas. Explain that the problem needs to start with 'If' so that the solution can follow.
● Encourage the children to be funny, but stress that stories cannot be rude or unkind about anybody.

Differentiation
This can be played as a picture game to make misfits. The children can draw a hat, head, upper body, legs and feet. But when the children fold the paper they must put little connecting lines to show where the picture should continue.

AGE RANGE 7–11

SUMMARY
Children play detective as they try to decipher codes.

Codes

What you need
Copies of the 'Codes (1) and (2)' photocopiable sheets on pages 56 and 57 (enough for one between two or three); pens or pencils; paper.

What to do
● Give each pair or three a copy of the photocopiable pages with the codes on.
● Explain to the children that they should decipher the coded questions. The keys are given below, but encourage the children to see if they can decipher the codes without them first.
● The children can compete to see who can be first to decipher the codes.
● Challenge the children to take turns to write down the answers to the questions in code before the key is written up on the board.
● Ask the children to take turns to write questions for each other, using one of the listed codes. The other(s) can answer in the same code, or use a different one.
● If the children feel confident with the codes, they can make up a code each and write down questions for each other to answer. Or they could make up a code together and write down some coded questions. Then pairs or threes can swap with one another and try to decode and answer each other's questions.

Code solutions
A The letters in each word have been reversed.
B Numbers instead of letters of the alphabet have been used (A=1, Z=26).
C The words have been broken and joined in the wrong places.
D 'Oho' has been inserted after every vowel.
E The numbers 1 to 9 and x and xx have been used to signify the letters of the alphabet:

	1	2	3	4	5	6	7	8	9
	A	B	C	D	E	F	G	H	I
X	J	K	L	M	N	O	P	Q	R
XX	S	T	U	V	W	X	Y	Z	

F 'Nuffun' has been inserted after the first vowel in every word.
G Exchange the last and the first letter in each word.
H Use 1 for A, 2 for E, 3 for I, 4 for O and 5 for U.

Ground rules
Encourage the children to work together and to have fun discovering and creating new codes to use.

Differentiation
Those children who cannot make up a new code can write questions using one of the codes listed on the photocopiable sheets for another pair to answer.

AGE RANGE 5–11

SUMMARY
Dragons compete for zones on a ladder.

Puff

What you need
Copies of the 'Puff' photocopiable sheet on page 58 (enough for one between two or three); colouring pencils; small screwed-up pieces of paper.

What to do
● The photocopiable page is taped to the table.
● There are three dragons on each rung of the ladder, and the players choose a column of dragons each. If there are only two players, they ignore the third dragon.
● Colin and Paul are playing. They place their piece of paper at the bottom edge of the photocopiable page.
● They each take it in turns to blow the paper up the ladder.
● When it comes to rest between the lines of the ladder they colour in one segment of their dragon there, starting with the legs and front, then the body, wings and tail, and finally the head. They each choose a specific colour to use throughout the game.
● When one of them has completed a dragon, by colouring in its head last, the other player's dragon on the same rung of the ladder becomes void and cannot be completed.
● For example, Colin lands on the top rung of the ladder, so he colours a dragon's feet and front in purple. Paul lands on the second rung and colours a dragon's feet and front in red. The game continues. Colin's paper lands on the top rung where he and Paul have both completed the legs and bodies of their dragons. He completes the head and Paul's dragon cannot now be completed.
● The player who completes the most dragons, and thus has the most rungs, wins.

Ground rules
● The children have only one puff of breath to blow the piece of paper on each turn. Counters and coins can be shoved instead, using one finger and nudging from the side, rather than putting a finger on the top.
● The children can only colour a segment of a dragon if the paper lands between the rungs of the ladder. If it touches a line, or goes off the top or the edges, it does not count and they may not have another try until their next turn.

Differentiation
This is an easy game for all ages to play. To make it more challenging, the paper has to stop on the dragon segment that the players want to colour in, rather than just landing between the rungs of the ladder.

AGE RANGE 7–11

SUMMARY
One child illustrates the word parts and another guesses the complete word.

Partwords

What you need
Copies of the 'Partwords' photocopiable sheet on page 59; pencil or pens; paper.

What to do
● Give each pair or three a copy of the photocopiable sheet. They can use the lists of words to help them, and can also think of their own words.
● Karen and Stevie work in a pair. Karen is the illustrator first. She thinks of a word that is made up of two shorter words, for example 'cowboy'.
● She draws a cow.
● Stevie looks at her picture and tries to guess the complete word. He has three guesses. If he guesses 'cowboy' when Karen has only drawn the first picture he gets ten points.
● If he does not, Karen draws the second part of the word: 'boy'.
● Stevie has three more guesses. He has to guess the complete word and Karen must not give him clues by telling him if his guess is correct. She can only say he is correct if he guesses the whole word correctly. If he does, he gets five points.
● If he still can't guess the word, Karen illustrates the complete word and draws a cowboy. Stevie gets two points for guessing now.
● Then it is Stevie's turn.
● If three children are playing, they have two guesses on their turn and each takes a turn at being the illustrator.

Ground rules
● Encourage the children to draw good pictures for each other rather than trying to make it hard by drawing badly, because they will then do this back to each other and spoil the game.
● The children can draw either part of the word first. So Karen might have drawn the boy first, and then the cow. The complete word is drawn last.
● The illustrator should not help by telling the other children if they have guessed the pictures illustrating part of the word correctly. They can only say *Correct!* when the complete word is guessed correctly.
● Illustrators can use arrows and other indicators in diagrams of abstract words, but cannot write any words.

Differentiation
The lists of words on the photocopiable sheet are suitable for different age groups. Words such as 'outwit' will be much harder to illustrate and to guess. The play leader can ask older children to use words from the hardest list.

PHOTOCOPIABLE

Finger puppet soaps

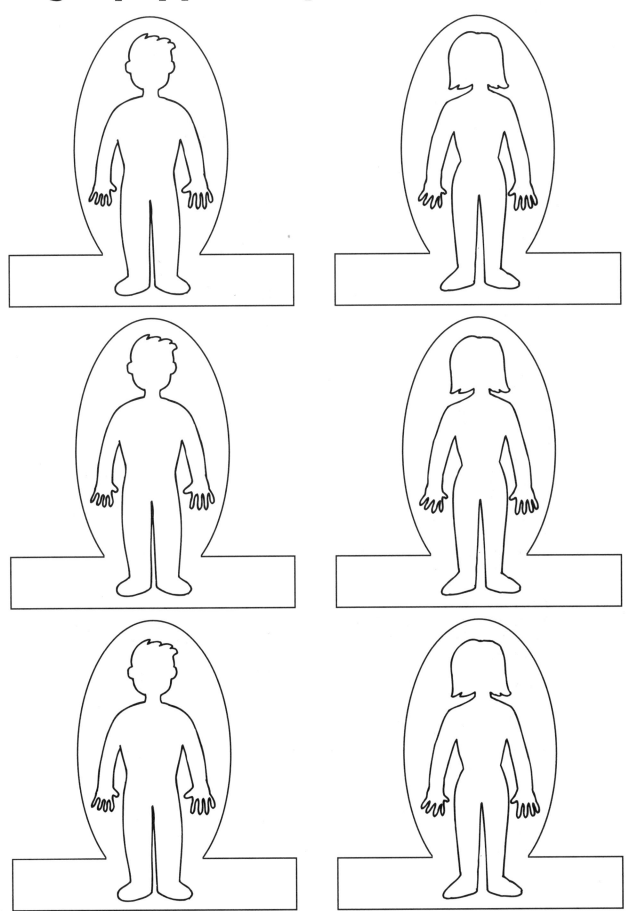

Codes (1)

Section A

Tahw era ruoy seman?

Od uoy evah yna step dna fi os tahw era yeht?

Eman ruoy etiruovaf trops.

Section B

23, 8, 1, 20.   9,19.   25, 15, 21, 18.   20, 5, 1, 3, 8, 5, 18, 19.   14, 1, 13, 5?
23, 18, 9, 20, 5.   4, 15, 23, 14.   20, 8, 5.   14, 1, 13, 5.   15, 6.   25, 15, 21, 18.   6,
1, 22, 15, 21, 18, 9, 20, 5.   19, 15, 14, 7.
23, 8, 1, 20.   3, 15, 12, 15, 21, 18.   1, 18, 5.   25, 15, 21, 18.   3, 12, 1, 19, 19, 18,
15, 15, 13.   23, 1, 12, 12, 19?

Section C

Wha tdi dyo uha vefo rlun chtod ay?

Wri tedo wnth enam eso ffiv echi ldre ninyo urclass.

Na meyo urfa vour itete levisi onpro gram me.

Section D

Whaohot iohos yoohouohor beohost toohoy oohor gaohomeoho?

Wriohoteoho doohown theoho naohomeohos oohof aoholl theoho chioholdreohon
aohot yoohouohor taohobleoho.

Whaohot aohoreoho yoohouohor hoohobbiohoeohos?

Codes (2)

Section E

5xx 8 1 2xx / 9 1xx / 7xx 6x 3xx 9x / 6 1 4xx 6x 3xx 9x 9 2xx 5 /
3 6x 3x 6x 3xx 9x?
5xx 8 1 2xx / 4 9 4 / 7xx 6x 3xx / 5 1 2xx / 6 6x 9x /
2 9x 5 1 2x 6 1 1xx 2xx / 2xx 6x 4 1 7xx?
5xx 9x 9 2xx 5 / 4 6x 5xx 5x / 2xx 8 5 / 5x 1 4x 5 / 6x 6 / 7xx 6x 3xx 9x/
7x 1 9x 2xx 5x 5 9x.

Section F

Inuffunt inuffuns funuffunn tonuffun senuffunnd senuffuncret menuffunssages
winuffunth conuffundes.

Thenuffun Monuffunrse Conuffunde wanuffuns inuffunnvented by Sanuffunmuel FB
Monuffunrse.

Yonuffunu canuffunn unuffunse dinuffunfferent conuffunloured senuffunquences
tonuffun manuffunke anuffun conuffunde.

Section G

Yhw ton eavh a koteboon hace, hitw rouy eodc seyk dna reat tuo sheets, ot eritw
sessagem ot rouy drienf.

A eimpls eodc si ot tup dolourec slantp ni rouy window; der rof ranged, erango rof
eb larefuc dna nreeg rof rntee.

Uoy nac od eht eams yb gsinu gashinw ganginh no a einl.

Section H

Th2 f1c2 4f w1tch2s 4r cl4cks c1n b2 5s2d t4 sh4w th2 s2m1ph4r2 1lph1b2t.
M1k2 5p 1 symb4l f4r 21ch l2tt2r 4f th2 1lph1b2t 1nd g3v2 1 c4py t4 1 fr32nd.
Try 5s3ng th2 mors2 cod2 3n d3ff2r2nt w1ys. For 3nst1nc2, b45nc3ng 1 b1ll.

▲SCHOLASTIC

Puff

Wet Playtimes BRIGHT IDEAS

Partwords

● These words will give you plenty of ideas for other words you can use for this game.

Easy	Hard	Hardest
Bookworm	Bowman	Bridesmaid
Candlestick	Bulldoze	Budget
Carpet	Buttercup	Content
Cowboy	Carrot	Cutlass
Fireguard	Daylight	Errant
Flagpole	Earthworm	Outwit
Foxglove	Eyebrow	Firework
Gooseberry	Hammock	Funfair
Hairclip	Homesick	Gauntlet
Handbag	Impact	Girlfriend
Honeycomb	Mainland	Heartfelt
Lighthouse	Mobbed	Impart
Lipstick	Moonbeam	Justice
Starfish	Primrose	Marshmallow
Postbox	Rampage	Mincemeat
Rainbow	Restrain	Napkin
Rosehip	Seaside	Plankton
Sandcastle	Songbird	Pumpkin
Saucepan	Stableboy	Railway
Sobbed	Stagecoach	Rampart
Suitcase	Sweetcorn	Sandalwood
Sunhat	Understand	Superhuman
Wallflower	Waterfall	Usage
Woodlice	Windmill	Whirlpool

CHAPTER 5

Physical fun

AGE RANGE 5–11

SUMMARY
Running around, body contact and lots of laughter for everybody.

Body parts

What you need
A large, clear space.

What to do
● Children run or walk around (depending on the environment) until the play leader calls out two body parts: *Head to knee.*
● The children stop and have to find a partner as quickly as possible, touching their different body parts together. Polly pairs up with Charlie and he bends to put his head against her knee.
● The play leader shouts *Go*, and the children move around again.
● The play leader then calls *Ear to back.* Polly and Charlie have to find different partners, so Polly puts her ear against Bianca's back.
● Charlie pairs with Colin, but they are the last pair to join up, so they go out of the game.
● If there is an odd number of children, one can be the play leader or the children can join up in twos and threes.

Ground rules
● The children should move around the room, either by walking or running, so that they do not deliberately hover near a friend they want to join up with.
● Children have to change partners or threes on their next turn so that they cannot keep joining with the same friends.
● The last pair or three to join up go out of the game.
● Alternatively, the game can be played just to let off steam and have fun without these elimination rules.

Differentiation
Some children may be embarrassed to do certain moves – cheek to cheek for example. The play leader will have to decide whether to use these and eject players who don't do them, or choose moves that they will be happy to play.

A harder version of the game for older groups, is for the play leader to call out criteria like height, birth date, birth month, shoe size or hair length. All the children have to line up in the order of the specified criteria.

A similar game is for the play leader to call out numbers between one and a number that the class size is divisible by. Children have to get into groups of this size.

AGE RANGE 5–11

SUMMARY
Jumping forwards and backwards
is harder than it seems.

River bank

What you need
A large, clear space; a thin line on the floor (this could be the edge of a carpet, a long rope or a chalked line).

What to do
● The children stand in a row behind the line on the floor.
● The 'river' is over the line and the 'bank' is behind it, so the children are standing on the bank.
● Anoushka is the play leader. She says *In the river*, and all the children jump over the line. Then she says *On the bank* and they jump back behind the line.
● She varies the order in which she calls these so that the children get confused, jumping when they shouldn't or staying still when they should jump.
● For example, she says *In the river* and the children jump over the line. She says *In the river* again, and Ellie and Kadie jump back onto the bank and are out.
● The idea is to gradually catch all the children out.
● Children who are out of the game can help by watching the other players to see if they make the wrong move.

Ground rules
● The play leader must call 'on' the bank or 'in' the river and cannot confuse the other children by saying 'in' the bank or 'on' the river. However, they can speed up, slow down, alternate or repeat the same instruction to try to get the other children out.
● The children should not touch the line with their feet. Their bodies should be over it or behind it on each turn. If they have a foot in each area they are out.

Differentiation
Younger children can step backwards and forwards, and then progress to jumping if they find this too easy. They may like to hold hands, which allows them to help each other.

AGE RANGE 5–11

SUMMARY
Children answer true or false by running to each end of the hall.

Running quiz

What you need
A large, clear space (for example, a hall); the 'Running quiz (1) and (2)' photocopiable sheets on pages 70 and 71.

What to do
● The children stand in the middle of the hall.
● The areas at each end are designated as 'true' and 'false'.
● The play leader reads out the true and false statements on the photocopiable sheets.
● The children run to the area that represents the answer that they think is correct.
● Then the play leader tells them which answer was correct, and they return to the middle of the hall for the next statement.
● The play leader can divide the class into two groups and give a point to the side with the most children opting for the correct answer. To make this simple the groups need to pre-exist. For example, girls versus boys, house teams or class groups.
● Alternatively, those children who choose the wrong answer can go out of the game.

Ground rules
● The children have to choose a true or false answer and go to that area. If they don't know, they should guess. Children who do not choose should either lose points or go out of the game.
● The children may not pull a friend with them or say the answer out loud.
● The children will dither and change their minds, and can do this provided they are not trying to influence others. They are not allowed to tell anybody what they think the answer is. The play leader can count down from five and then the children have to stick to the area that they have chosen.

Differentiation
A funny variation for smaller areas is to write 'true' or 'false' in marker pen on sheets of newspaper and lay them on the floor. The children have to squash together on these to signify their answer. If space is limited, the children can stand to signify 'true' and sit down for 'false'.

Questions that are suitable for children of different ages and abilities are listed on the photocopiable sheets.

AGE RANGE 5–11

SUMMARY
A mad run-around game that is great fun.

Hoop he

What you need
Hoops (at least half the amount than there are children).

What to do
● This game works best with around 10 to 15 children. The class could be divided into groups to take turns to play, or the room could be divided so that two games run simultaneously.
● Place the hoops randomly over the floor.
● Jack is 'It'. He chases the other children and tries to touch them. Whoever he touches becomes 'It' instead.
● The hoops are 'home'. 'It' cannot touch anybody who is in one.
● Only one child at a time can occupy a hoop. If another child enters, then the first child must get out and go to another.

● For example, Jack chases Laura, who runs away and jumps into a hoop that is occupied by Sasha. Sasha gets out and runs towards a hoop occupied by Javed, while being chased by Jack. She jumps into Javed's hoop and Javed gets out. Jack touches him and he becomes 'It'. Now he is after Jack, who runs away and jumps into Clare's hoop. She gets out and runs away, and so on.
● The game usually ends when everybody is puffed out.

Ground rules
● Only one child can occupy a hoop at a time and they must vacate it when somebody else enters.
● 'It' cannot enter the hoops.
● The children may need a breather in this game. Anybody who needs a rest can sit down in a hoop and nobody can enter it. However, they must be sitting properly on their bottom rather than kneeling or squatting. If they do this too often the play leader should ask them to sit out of the game for their rest!
● If 'It' gets tired he should call out *Hoop he* and sit down. Everyone else must sit down until he stands up to resume the game.

Differentiation
This game can be played with two children being 'It' at the same time, or by asking the children to jump or hop between hoops. It can be made harder by gradually removing hoops. Children can go out of the game when they are touched, while 'It' stays in place.

AGE RANGE 5–11

SUMMARY
Children have to work together to stop 'Chuff' jumping onto their train.

Chuff

What you need
A large, clear space.

What to do
● One child is chosen to be 'Chuff'.
● The other children get together in pairs or threes. One child stands behind another and holds their waist, forming a mini-train.
● Explain that 'Chuff' is a loose carriage and needs a train to join. Chuff will try to join on by holding the waist of a child who is at the back of a train.
● The children have to dodge around to try to stop Chuff joining on to their train.
● When Chuff manages to join a train, he shouts *Chuff*. The leader of the train he has joined leaves to become Chuff, and tries to hop onto the back of another train.

Ground rules
● The children are only to hold each other around the waist. Explain that in a game like this it is easy to grab clothes and tear them, so they must be careful or other children will not want them in their train.
● If a train breaks, the child at the back of it becomes Chuff and the original Chuff takes their place on that train.
● This is a fast-moving game and children will need to be able to stop and catch their breath. 'Station' is the password that children can use if they need a breather. It is also useful for the play leader to use if they think that the children need a break. If anybody calls 'Station' everybody must stop immediately and sit down. Anybody who does not stop must sit out when everybody else plays the next round.

Differentiation
Longer trains of three or four children make it easier for Chuff to hop on the back, which will help younger children. If the children are playing in a hall, they could mark out tracks to follow like real trains.

AGE RANGE 5–11

SUMMARY
A live obstacle course.

Jeopardy

What you need
A large, clear space; a blindfold.

What to do
● Carlos and Nadia are chosen
as the players. Four children,
Stacey, Chi Han, Jo and
Steven are the arches and all
the other children are trees.
● The children who are
trees spread out across
the hall with their arms
outstretched.
● The children who are
the arches join hands in pairs
and raise their hands up high
to make an arch shape. The two
arches should be a distance apart
from each other – one near the beginning
and one near the end of the course. If it is a
large hall, there could be another arch in the middle.
● Nadia is blindfolded at one side of the room and Carlos is on the other. Carlos calls
instructions which Nadia follows. He has to get her from the beginning of the course to
the end. She has to go underneath the arches, avoiding contact with the trees.
● When Nadia has completed the course, two other children are chosen to play. When
one of them is blindfolded the children who are trees and arches move to alter the
layout of the landscape.
● After everyone has had a turn, players who completed the course properly play
again. This time the other player in each pair is blindfolded. The remaining pairs
compete against each other until there is a final winner.

Ground rules
● The children who are playing as trees or arches can rest their arms when the
blindfolded player is not nearby.
● If the blindfolded player bumps into a tree, they and their partner are out and
another pair are chosen to play. However, it does not matter if they touch an arch while
trying to go underneath it.
● Children who are watching should keep their voices down so that the blindfolded
player can hear the instructions from their partner.
● Encourage the children to give pairs a clap when they finish – whether they
complete the course or not.

Differentiation
Instead of walking, the blindfolded player can crawl across the course. In this case, the
trees can sit down with outstretched arms, or curl up and become boulders instead.

AGE RANGE 5–11

SUMMARY
A story and physical fun
combined.

Turning tales

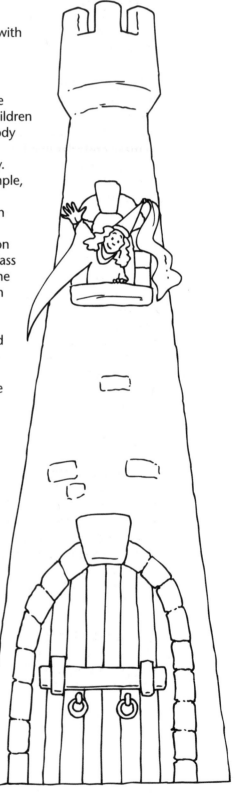

What you need
A clear space; the 'Turning tales (1) and (2)' photocopiable
sheets on pages 72 and 73, or an easy book of short stories with
frequently repeated words.

What to do
● The class should be divided into three or four groups. The
groups spread out and sit down on the floor. Suggest the children
stretch out their arms to make sure they do not touch anybody
else before they sit down.
● The play leader explains that they are going to tell a story.
● Each group is given a key word to listen out for. For example,
sun, *rainbow*, *kitten* and *tree*.
● When the groups hear their key word, they stand up, turn
around and sit down.
● There are also key action words (listed above the stories on
photocopiable pages 72 and 73) for all the children in the class
to respond to. For instance, *miaow* (children have to make the
sound); *climb* (children pretend to climb); and *sleep* (children
pretend to be asleep).
● The play leader reads: *Once there was a kitten who was
sleeping on a cushion in the sun.* The group with the key word
'kitten' jump up, turn around, sit down and then pretend to
sleep. The group with the key word 'sun' pretend to sleep
and then jump up, turn around and sit down. The rest of the
children pretend to sleep.
● As the play leader proceeds to tell the story, the children
have to remember to respond as fast as possible in the right
order. It gets hectic and hilarious!

Ground rules
● The children must be quiet so that they can hear the
story, although the play leader might need to increase their
volume as the giggling gets louder.
● The game is usually played for fun, but the last to
respond to a key word could go out of the game so that
players are gradually eliminated.

Differentiation
Instead of standing up, turning around and sitting down,
the children could play the game sitting in a large circle.
Children hearing their key word, jump up, run around
the outside of the circle and back to their place.
The two stories for this game are suitable for longer and
shorter time spans. Play leaders can choose their own
story books or make up stories, delegating key words
accordingly.

AGE RANGE 5–11

SUMMARY
An exciting variation of an old-fashioned favourite.

Searchlight

What you need
A torch; two cones or markers; covers – old curtains or sheets (optional).

What to do
● Set up the room first. If there are tables or chairs, cover them with curtains or sheets to make obstacles that the children can hide behind. Put two cones or markers about four steps apart and roughly two metres from the end of the room. Playing this game with the blinds or curtains closed adds to the fun.

● If tables, chairs or covers are not available, divide the class into two groups who can take turns to play and to be the obstacles. If the children are the obstacles, they should sit, stand or crouch down in pairs or groups to make interesting shapes for the others to hide behind.

● The play leader stands behind the gap between the markers with a torch.

● The children start at the end of the hall and have to creep or crawl across it while the play leader moves the torch beam around. If the torch beam rests on a moving child they are out of the game

● The aim is for the children to cross the boundary – the area between the markers.

● The game continues until all the children have crossed the boundary or are out.

● If there are two groups, the next group plays while the first becomes the obstacles.

Ground rules
● Once the children have part of their body across the boundary, even if it is just a hand, they are home.

● The first across the boundary in each game could become the play leader with the torch for the next game.

● If the children are obstacles they must stay still. They are not allowed to be moving obstacles.

● If tables or chairs are covered, the children have to be careful that they don't pull the covers off.

Differentiation
The game can be played with the children going back to the start again if they are caught moving when the torch beam rests on them.

AGE RANGE 5–11

SUMMARY
Children are predators competing with each other to capture the most prey.

Jungle rumble

What you need
A large, clear space.

What to do
● The children stand in a line at one end of the hall. They are jungle animals.
● Farzhad and Ann are chosen to be the predators. Farzhad decides to be a lion and Ann is a cheetah. They stand in their 'lairs' on either side of the hall.
● When the play leader calls *Jungle rumble*, all the 'animals' run from one end of the hall to the other. The 'lion' and the 'cheetah' have to try to touch them before they get to the other side.
● Any children who are touched by a predator have to go to the lair of whoever caught them.
● When all the children have been caught the play leader counts the animals that the predators have captured. Farzhad the lion has captured 12 children, while Ann the cheetah has 18. Therefore, Ann is declared the best predator for that game and chooses two children to be the next predators.

Ground rules
● The predators can only capture children when they are running from one end of the hall to the other. When they reach the other end they are out of bounds. Children can touch the wall to show they are home or a boundary can be marked for them to cross to safety.
● Predators must touch the children to capture them, and must not pull or drag them. Children who are touched by one of the predators must go and sit in their lair. If there is a dispute, the play leader decides whether they were caught and by whom.

Differentiation
Four predators, two working together on either side, makes the game easier for younger children. Encourage younger players to decide which jungle animals they are and to act like this animal during the game.

Wet Playtimes BRIGHT IDEAS

AGE RANGE 5–11

SUMMARY
A vigorous, popular team game.

Balloon bash tournament

What you need
A large, clear space; a packet of balloons.

What to do
● Teams should be five to eight a side, but two or three games can be played at the same time, with play leaders or referees in charge of each.
● Teams of equal number sit in a row facing each other, with about a step's gap between the teams.
● The play leader drops a balloon in between the teams. They have to try to score a goal by batting it over the heads of the opposing team so that it lands on the floor behind them.
● The play leader keeps count of the score. The first team to score five goals wins.
● If there are two or three games running, then winning and losing teams can swap over and play each other so that there is an overall winner.

Ground rules
● Define the areas at each end of the teams in which the balloon will be declared 'out'. Use markers if necessary.
● The children must sit down. If their bottoms leave the floor, they must sit out until the next goal is scored (by either side).
● After each goal, the play leader should drop the balloon in the middle of the teams again, varying the position, so that all players have a chance to start first.
● After each game, another play leader should be chosen so the previous one can play in the next game.
● If a balloon bursts, another one should be supplied with no penalties to either side.

Differentiation
Younger children will need to sit closer to each other. Get them to touch feet with their opposite team member. They will find it impossible to stay on their bottoms, so allow them to kneel down as long as they do not crawl around the floor after the balloon.

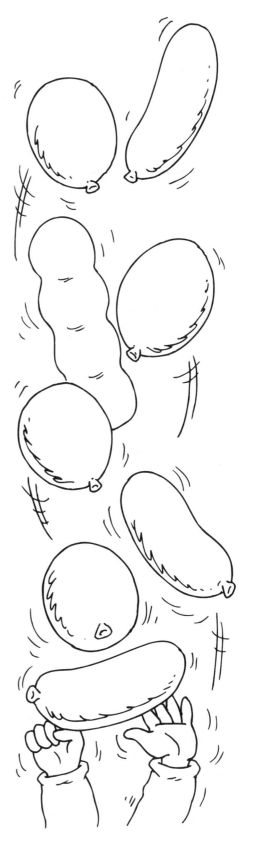

Running quiz (1)

Very easy statements

T A cow has four legs.

F A slipper is somebody that slips over.

F Little Bo Peep looks after cows.

T Honey is made by bees.

T An igloo is a house made of ice.

F In the Bible, Goliath built an ark to escape from the floods.

T A snail has a shell.

F Paper is made from a type of seaweed.

T Bananas are yellow.

F Wool comes from kittens.

T Postmen deliver letters and parcels.

T Polo is a sport.

T A snowdrop is a flower.

T A baker's shop sells bread.

T Midges are insects.

F A tutu is a type of hammer.

T Mars is a planet.

F Winnie the Pooh is a dog.

Easy statements

F JK Rowling wrote 'Alice in Wonderland'.

T Bacon comes from a pig.

F A cybercafe is where people take their cyberpets for a snack.

T Squares have four sides and four corners.

T A hurricane is a very strong wind.

F A chihuahua is a small cat.

T Old Macdonald had a farm.

F You need a net and a shuttlecock to play ping pong.

T Koala bears live in Australia.

F A jukebox is a box which contains fake jewellery.

T A fool can mean a type of dessert.

T Buckingham Palace is in London.

F A nightjar is a type of lantern.

T A nun's dress is called a habit.

F Another name for a horse chestnut is an acorn.

F New York is known as the Big Hamburger.

T Chocolate is made from the cocoa bean.

F A cranefly is known as a Granny Legit.

T Shrove Tuesday is known as Pancake Day.

F A tomato is a vegetable.

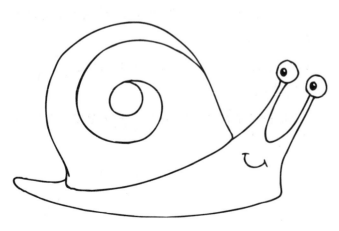

Running quiz (2)

Hard statements

T A quiche is a savoury flan.

T Angling is the same as fishing.

F Scientist Einstein's first name was Edward.

T A hexagon has six sides.

F Basil, rosemary and tarragon are types of tree.

T A paw paw is a fruit.

T The Woolly Mammoth is extinct.

F A wimple is a weak and weedy person.

F Toffee Lane is a song made famous by the Beatles.

F "A bird in the hand saves nine", is a proverb.

T An otter is a mammal.

T Shakespeare's first name was William.

T Claustrophobia is a fear of confined spaces.

F The river Nile is in New Zealand.

T Philately is another word for stamp collecting.

T JRR Tolkien wrote 'The Lord of the Rings'.

F Laurel and Hardy were inventors.

F Foliage is a type of cereal.

T A quiver would contain arrows.

F Spain is an island.

Harder statements

T A baby hare is called a leveret.

T Dinosaur means terrible lizard.

F The letter "H" in HGV stands for Hard.

T Rennet is used in cheese making.

T Smog is a mixture of smoke and fog.

F A Puffing Ventris is a type of insect.

F Calais is the capital of France.

F Someone with a leap year birthday is called a Leapovian.

T Hercule Poirot is a fictional Belgian detective.

T Gelatine is obtained from animal bones.

T Sweet William is a type of flower.

F Potholing is a type of outdoor cooking over a hole.

T Numismatics is the study of coins.

F Muscovado is a small African bird.

F A talisman is a door-to-door salesman.

T Dowsing is another word for water divining.

F A kimono is a Japanese rice cracker.

F The Mr Men books were written by Roald Dahl.

Turning Tales (1)

Group key words: love   grin   tower   princess
Class key word: Fangtoosely Woosely Fing

The Fangtoosely Woosely Fing
Once a lone <u>princess</u> lived in a very high <u>tower</u>,
She was very bored so her face was rather sour.
No prince came near to visit, because of her grumpy looks,
So she sat in her <u>tower</u> reading lots of storybooks.

Now in the forest quite close by there lurked a scary thing,
Mustard yellow with googly eyes, the **Fangtoosely Woosely Fing**.
One day it was looking for fat slugs to eat and saw the <u>princess</u> above,
and the **Fangtoosely Woosely Fing** fell deeply and madly in <u>love</u>.

With a cheesy <u>grin</u> he sat under her <u>tower</u> and sang all the songs that he knew,
The <u>princess</u> thought that the noise was awful, but did not know what to do.
The cook, the butler, the king and the maids came out to see the strange thing,
When they saw the **Fangtoosely Woosely Fing**, they all started to <u>grin</u>.

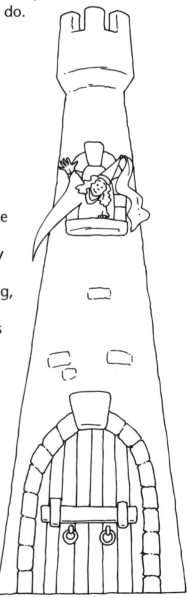

He looked so funny under the <u>tower</u> all goofy with <u>love</u> and passion,
And **Fangtoosely Woosely Fings** don't dress well or wear the height of fashion.
So he had on a blazer in blue and pink and a crumpled hat of wool,
And he thought he looked fantastic, but he actually looked rather a fool.

But strangely the <u>princess</u> looked down from the <u>tower</u> and her face broke into a <u>grin</u>,
For he looked so funny, the badly dressed, <u>love</u>lorn **Fangtoosely Woosely Fing**,
He looked up and sighed with a tear in his eye and said, 'Marry me darling, please do.'
She looked down with a <u>grin</u> and said, 'If we wed, I'll choose your clothes for you.'

He said, 'Anything, but can I still sing for I think I'm rather a hit.'
And everybody cheered and agreed – well, he was a bit.
So the <u>love</u>struck pair got wed one day and although the <u>princess</u> was hoping,
He did not turn into a handsome prince, but she did not start moping.
She was far too busy making slug stew and buying cool clothes for him,
And he was a very happy contented **Fangtoosely Woosely Fing**.

© *Deborah Sharpe*

Wet Playtimes **BRIGHT IDEAS**

Turning Tales (2)

Group key words: elephant   queen   lion   Albert
Class key words: jungle   animals   king

Queen of the jungle

Once there was a **jungle** hidden on top of a town centre car park. The car park owner did not like being surrounded by concrete, so he had made the top level into a **jungle**. Cars could not drive further than Level 7 and the **jungle**, complete with **animals**, was imported from Africa and put on Level 8.

The car park owner chose an <u>elephant</u> called Stella to be <u>queen</u> of the <u>jungle</u>.

Stella the <u>elephant</u> made a great <u>queen</u> and the **animals** in the **jungle** were content, apart from <u>Albert Lion</u>'s wife, Hetty. Hetty thought that her husband, <u>Albert</u>, should be **king** and nagged continuously.

'You should be **king** of the **jungle**, it's always a <u>lion</u> who's **king**. Get the other **animals** on your side and overthrow the <u>queen</u>. **Animals** in other **jungles** would laugh if they knew we had a <u>queen</u> <u>elephant</u> instead of a **king** <u>lion</u>.'

<u>Albert</u> was too lazy to care about being **king**, but Hetty went on and on and on.

'All right, I'll speak to her majesty,' he said.

He wandered off to find <u>Queen</u> Stella the <u>elephant</u> who was standing in the shade of a tall tree.

'Hello Your Majesty,' he said bowing low. 'May I have a word?'

'I always have time for my subjects,' said <u>Queen</u> Stella. 'What can I do for you <u>Albert Lion</u>?

'Um, are you happy being <u>queen</u> of the **jungle**? Wouldn't you rather be an ordinary <u>elephant</u>?' he asked.

'I'm very happy, thank you for asking,' <u>Queen</u> Stella replied. 'I think it is far more sensible to have an <u>elephant</u> as **king** or <u>queen</u>, if you don't mind me saying. We are huge, heavy and very strong, but we are also very peaceful.'

'Oh. Well, the thing is, it's not me you understand, but some **animals** think I should be **king**.'

'Then you had better see the car park owner, because it is his **jungle**,' she said.

'Where will I find him, Your Majesty?'

'On one of the lower levels through the red doors marked 'No Exit',' <u>Queen</u> Stella the <u>elephant</u> said.

'But we're not supposed to go through there. That door is so that he can visit the **jungle**,' <u>Albert Lion</u> said.

'Well, if you're happy to wait until he appears I'll tell him you want a word. But it might be days – or even weeks – if he's busy,' she said.

'I think I'll risk the door,' <u>Albert Lion</u> said as he saw his wife lurking in the bushes. 'Thank you, Your Majesty.'

'Not at all,' <u>Queen</u> Stella the <u>elephant</u> said.

<u>Albert Lion</u> went straight to the edge of the **jungle** where tall trees hid the red doors with 'No Exit' on them that led to the car park. He went through them and looked around for the car park owner. There was no sign of him, so <u>Albert</u> walked down a level just as a car was coming up.

Albert Lion had never seen cars before so he thought it was a fierce animal and turned and fled back to the **jungle**.

The people in the car screamed and the driver slammed his brakes on, but the lion vanished so quickly they decided that it must have been a trick of the light.

'I have just seen the most ferocious animal you can imagine,' Albert Lion told all the **animals** on his return.

'Did you fight it? Did you win?' the **animals** asked.

'Er, yes, I did and now you won't be bothered by it,' he lied, hoping that the awful creature would not come up to their **jungle**. 'Now surely I deserve to be **king**?'

'Yes, you've vanquished the enemy, you should be **king**,' the **animals** agreed, just as Queen Stella the elephant strolled up to them. The **animals** bowed.

'Your Majesty,' they said, and then nudged and poked each other. They were all scared to tell her that they thought Albert Lion should be **king**. It was Hetty who stepped forward

'Your Majesty. My husband, Albert Lion, has just destroyed a fearsome beast who was trying to invade our **jungle**,' she said.

'Have you indeed Albert Lion,' Queen Stella the elephant said. 'What beast was this?'

'Absolutely terrifying,' Albert Lion said. 'Huge shining eyes, a ferocious roar, smoke coming out of its… ahem… '

'You must be brave to have destroyed such a beast,' Queen Stella said. 'What did you do?'

'Erm, I growled,' he said.

'Was that enough to scare such a ferocious beast away, Albert Lion?' she asked.

'Erm, no, then I… '

'He fought it,' Hetty chipped in.

'That was brave of you,' Queen Stella said. 'How?'

'I scratched it with my claws, and I bit and tore its flesh until it ran away,' Albert lied.

'Oh dear, so it might recover and come to our **jungle** to get you. It might bring ferocious friends too,' Queen Stella the elephant said. 'It would have been wiser and safer for all of us if you had run away and hidden so that it did not see you. Now we could all be in danger.'

'Oh well. ' Albert Lion did not know what to say and the **animals** looked nervous and started grumbling.

'You've made it dangerous for all of us… What a stupid lion… Why did you have to fight it?' they mumbled.

'Anyway, I'd better go and have some lunch and a think about how to protect us all,' Queen Stella the elephant said. 'Unless anyone else has anything to say?'

'No, Your Majesty,' the **animals** said. They shoved past Albert Lion and walked off, leaving him with his wife Hetty.

'Now look what you've done,' she said. 'Why couldn't you…'

'SHUT UP!' Albert Lion roared, and Hetty was so surprised, she did!

© *Deborah Sharpe*

CHAPTER 6

Paper capers

AGE RANGE 5–11

SUMMARY
Attractive decorations that twirl
in the breeze.

Whirly snakes

What you need
Copies of the 'Whirly snakes' photocopiable sheet on page 85, copied onto thin card if possible (enough for one per child); colouring pens or pencils; scissors; cotton thread or wool; paperclips.

What to do
● Give each child a copy of the 'Whirly snakes' photocopiable sheet and the equipment to make the snakes.
● First, ask the children to colour in their snakes. Encourage them to think about different types of patterns as well as colours and to make theirs as bright and cheerful as possible.
● When they have finished, tell them they should carefully cut along the dotted lines. They will now have a spiral snake.
● Next, tell them they need to attach a piece of cotton thread to the head. They might need some help with this. The best way is to use a sharp pencil or compass to make a hole, and to thread cotton through, tying it in a knot on one side. Another way is to open up a paper clip and thread it through so the snake hangs from this, then cotton or wool can be attached to the paper clip.
● You can turn this wet playtime activity into a classroom display. Hang the snakes near a window or door so that they twirl in the breeze. You can hang strips of green tissue paper around the snakes to add to the theme.
● Small prizes or stickers could be awarded for the best decorated snake.

Differentiation
Young children will need help to cut out the snakes and attach the wool or cotton. If this is not possible, they could colour the snake and take it home so that their parents or carers can help.

Older children may prefer to make whirling decorations rather than snakes. Fluorescent pens, foil, sequins, tissue paper and magazines cut to make mosaic shapes can be glued on to make these really eye-catching. The spiral should be cut out before the decorations are added.

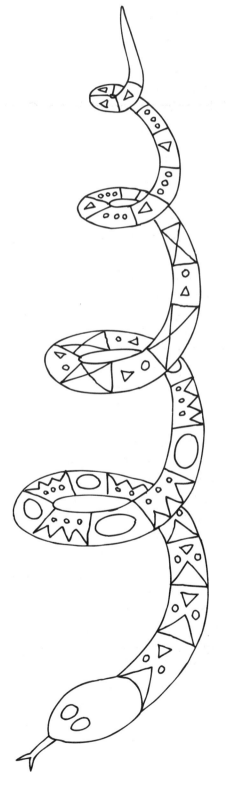

AGE RANGE 5–11

SUMMARY
Brightly coloured spinners for
the children to play with.

Spinners

What you need
Copies of the 'Spinners' photocopiable sheet on page 86, copied onto card (enough for
one per child); colouring pens or pencils; scissors; glue sticks; wool or string.

What to do
● Give each child a copy of the 'Spinners' photocopiable sheet and the equipment to
make the spinners.
● Ask the children to colour both discs on the photocopiable sheet, using lots of
different colours.
● The children should then carefully cut out the discs and stick them together, back to
back.
● Show the children how to punch a small hole through the centre (marked) with a
compass or pencil.
● Then tell them to measure out a length of wool or string about 50cm. Explain that
they should double it up and knot the ends together so that the doubled length is
around 25cm. Tell the children to thread the wool or string through the middle of the
disc, threading it from the opposite end to the knot.
● Show the children how to put their forefingers in each end of the string or wool and
turn the disc over a few times. They can play in pairs so that one child holds the string
at both ends, and the other turns the disc over. Then explain that they should pull
outwards to tighten the string.
● The disc will spin and the colours will swirl together.
● Adjustments to the size of the central hole may need to be made so that the disc
spins properly. Encourage the children to do this gradually so that they do not make the
hole too large, which will stop it working properly.
● After the children have enjoyed watching the colours swirling and comparing each
other's discs, suggest that they have competitions on their tables or in pairs to see
whose disc spins the longest.

Differentiation
Most children enjoy this activity, especially comparing the effects of the different colours
as they spin them afterwards. They can make several spinners to experiment with
different colours and patterns. Young children will need help with cutting and threading
the string through the middle of the discs.

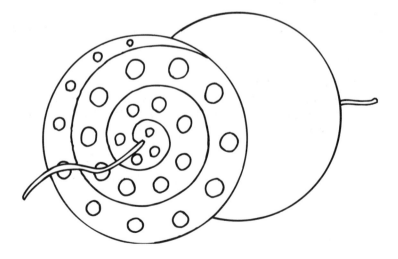

AGE RANGE 5–11

SUMMARY
Face templates let children experiment with different expressions and characters.

Freaky faces

What you need
Copies of the 'Freaky faces' photocopiable sheet on page 87 (enough for one per child); colouring pens or pencils; scissors.

What to do
● Give each child a copy of the 'Freaky faces' photocopiable sheet and the equipment to make the faces (the photocopiable sheet can be enlarged).
● The blank faces allow the children to experiment by drawing and colouring in lots of different characters.
● Explain to the children that they could draw lots of different expressions. For example, angry, happy, surprised, cruel, nervous, lost, thoughtful, laughing, crying, shouting, good, naughty, hopeful, singing, smirking, winking.
● Let the children decide if they want to experiment with different expressions or if they want to come up with a theme for the faces.
● Suggest that they may want to draw faces that represent a crowd of football supporters – with the

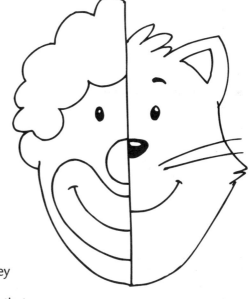

expressions that they might have if their team were winning or losing a match. Other ideas could be people watching a scary film, a romantic play, listening to a boring speech or all the guests at a wedding. The children will probably have lots of their own theme ideas too.
● Alternatively, suggest to the children that they create different characters. For example, an old person, a baby, Mum, Dad, teacher, judge, nurse, queen, king, pop star, witch, postman, firefighter or actor.
● Encourage the children to draw faces from different countries and cultural backgrounds.
● Try asking them to draw other children in the class. These would make a great display and allow everyone to compare the different ways that they have drawn each other.
● When all the faces are finished they can be cut out and assembled as a crowd scene on a giant classroom frieze.

Differentiation
Young children might need a smaller, specific idea to follow. For example, drawing the members of their family, the children around their table, a favourite story or the faces of all their cuddly toys.

AGE RANGE 5–11

SUMMARY
A popular, old-fashioned activity
revived for today's children.

Fashion show

What you need
Copies of the 'Fashion show (1)' photocopiable sheet on page 88, copied onto card,
and the 'Fashion show (2)' photocopiable sheet on page 89, copied onto paper
(enough for one per child or to share between two); colouring pens or pencils; scissors;
small bags or containers.

What to do
● Give each child or pair copies of the 'Fashion show (1) and (2)' photocopiable sheets
and the equipment to make the figures.
● Tell the children to colour in the figure on the 'Fashion show (1)' sheet, adding
features and hair. Then explain that they should carefully cut the figure out. To stand
it on its base, tell the children to cut the tabs on the feet where indicated, slot the tabs
into the base and stick the tabs underneath the base.
● Ask the children to colour in the clothes and accessories on both photocopiable
sheets and fit them onto their figure. The children will
have used different colours, patterns and styles, so they
can compare and try out each other's.

● Then the children can play a game. Put them into
pairs (or fours if they have shared the activity sheets
between two). Tell them to put all the clothes and
accessories into a bag or container. Explain that they
should take turns to take one and to put it onto their
figure. The first child or pair to have dressed their figure
is the winner.

Ground rules (for the fashion game)
● The completed figure should be wearing a hat, a top,
trousers, shoes and two accessories.
● If the children take out something that their figure
is already wearing, they can swap it if they think it looks
better, and put the other item back in the bag. However,
they may not have another turn in that round.
● This game could be played with more children (all
those on a particular table, for example) competing to
complete their figure.

Differentiation
To add interest, especially for older children, suggest they
add designer logos or colours of their favourite football
team. They could also make their figure look like a sports,
film, TV or pop star, or even themselves or another
friend. Suggest younger children colour in clothes that
are the easiest to cut out. They can also play the game
without accessories.

AGE RANGE 5–11

SUMMARY
The children can have a lot of fun making and characterizing balloons.

Balloon people

What you need
Copies of the 'Balloon people' photocopiable sheet on page 90, copied onto card (enough for one per child); one balloon per child (and some spare ones in case they burst); colouring pencils and felt-tipped pens; coloured and tissue paper; wool; card; sticky tape; glue; rolled-up newspapers.

What to do
● Give each child a copy of the 'Balloon people' photocopiable sheet, a balloon, and the equipment and materials to make the balloon people.
● Ask the children to colour in and cut out the feet on their photocopiable sheet. They can draw shoes or toes on the feet, or just simply colour them in with a single colour or using patterns. Explain that they need to cut the cross in the feet (where indicated) so they can slot their balloon into it.
● Next, tell them they should blow up their balloon and tie the end. The tied part should be pushed through the cross in the feet and taped down on the bottom side so that the balloon stands upright on its 'feet'. It should be pulled fairly tightly and slightly towards the back of the feet. The children may need a few attempts to do this properly.
● Explain that features should be added to the balloon by cutting out shapes in coloured paper and sticking or taping them on. Wool or strips of paper can be used for hair. Encourage the children to use felt-tipped colouring pens to add ears, facial hair, cheeks and eyebrows, as well as eyes, a nose and a mouth to really make the balloon people look exciting. However, point out that it's not a good idea to draw on the balloon people using pencils!
● Finally, they could line their balloon people up on the floor and, holding a rolled-up newspaper, flap it so that these race across the floor.

Differentiation
Young children will need help to fit their balloon to the feet, but it is such a great activity that play leaders should not let this put them off. Perhaps older, more capable children could be enlisted to go around and help. Alternatively, the activity could be pre-prepared, with the balloons being blown up and fitted to the feet in advance.

AGE RANGE 5–11

SUMMARY
Mini-footballers with finger legs so that the children can play table football.

Funny footballers

What you need
Copies of the 'Funny footballers' photocopiable sheet on page 91; colouring pens and pencils; scissors; A3 paper (optional).

What to do
● Give each child a copy of the 'Funny footballers' photocopiable sheet, colouring pens and pencils, and scissors.
● Ask the children to colour the characters in their favourite football team colours, or in their favourite colour, and cut them out. Explain that they should also cut around the dotted lines on the footballer's shorts to make two finger holes.
● Next, they should colour in and cut out the football boots.
● Show the children how to put their fingers through the holes in their footballer's shorts to become their legs. Using some rolled or double-sided sticky tape, or a dab from a glue stick, demonstrate how the football boots can be stuck to the nail of each finger.
● The children can mark out a pitch on A3 paper, or just mark goals on the table using tape, erasers, paper clips or paper. The ball can be a screwed-up piece of paper, a bead or a marble.
● Using their 'funny footballers', the children can play football against themselves or against a friend.
● Finally, pipe cleaners can be bent to go through each hole, and the football boots can be stuck on the ends of these so that all the funny footballers can go on display. The children could make a football frieze for the wall or they could stick thread to the back of their funny footballers' heads and create a hanging display.

Ground rules
If the 'ball' goes off the table onto the floor then the other team's funny footballer can kick it back onto the 'pitch' from the edge of the table. Apart from this, the children can decide how many rules from the real game to apply to their table game.

Differentiation
The footballers might be easy to cut out, but younger children may need help with making the finger holes.
   Instead of a game, the children can take turns to shoot with one of their funny footballers, while a friend's footballer acts as goalkeeper. It is quite fun for children to do this against themselves, with their own funny footballers on each hand.

AGE RANGE 5–8

SUMMARY
Sinister faces with moving eyes.

Spooky portraits

What you need
Copies of the 'Spooky portraits' photocopiable sheet on page 92; colouring pens and pencils; paper fasteners; scissors; string and a sheet (optional).

What to do
● Give each child a copy of the 'Spooky portraits' photocopiable sheet, colouring pens and pencils, paper fasteners and scissors.
● Explain to the children that they should add features to the face on the photocopiable sheet: mouth, ears, hair, nose. Tell them that the nose should be drawn around the small cross in the middle of the face, so that it is in the centre. Explain that they should not draw any eyes yet.
● Tell the children they can draw any kind of face or character for their spooky portrait, such as a witch or a vampire. Encourage them to add additional features, such as beards, moustaches, glasses and hats. When they have drawn their face explain that they should colour it in.
● Show the children how the eyeholes need to be cut out around the dotted lines.
● Next, ask the children to cut out the disc at the bottom of the page. Explain that they should draw and colour in two pairs of eyes where marked, in different colours. Suggest they draw a large and a small pair of eyes, or one pair looking one way and the other looking in the opposite direction.
● Demonstrate how the paper fastener goes through the central mark in the nose on the portrait and then through the central mark on the disc, which should be attached behind the portrait.
● Let them see that by turning the disc behind the portrait they can make the eyes move and change them to a different pair. Suggest they also take out the disc and look through the eyeholes themselves.
● It is fun to hang a washing line and sheet across the room, take the discs off the portraits and hang up half of them. Let some children stand behind the portraits while the others guess who is behind which portrait. Then they can swap over.

Differentiation
The children may need help to cut out and fasten the discs to the back of the portraits. These can be pre-prepared if necessary.

AGE RANGE 5–8

SUMMARY
Children decorate the fish and can then race them.

Flappy fish

What you need
Copies of the 'Flappy fish' photocopiable sheet on page 93 (enough for one per child); colouring pens and pencils; scissors; sequins, wool, tissue paper, glue (all optional); newspapers (optional); a sheet (optional).

What to do
● Give each child a copy of the 'Flappy fish' photocopiable sheet and the materials and equipment to make the fish.
● Tell the children to colour in their fish. As well as experimenting with different colours and patterns, they could also stick sequins, tissue paper and wool on to them.
● Encourage them to name their fish with fancy, fishy names like Slithery Silver or Wilfred the Water Wanderer.
● Next, explain that they need to cut out their fish and line them all up so that everyone can vote on which fish is the best decorated. The easiest way to do this is for the children to stand by the fish that they like best (they cannot choose their own).
● In pairs, groups or all together, let the children line up their fish in a row on a table or on the floor and race them by waving a folded sheet of newspaper at them or blowing them.
● The fish can also be used in a parachute game. The children should put their name on the back of their fish and throw them into the middle of the 'parachute' (or a large sheet). Explain to the children that they have to shake the parachute to try to eject them all and the last fish out of the parachute is the winner.
● Finally, the fish can be hung nose to tail around the room as an attractive decoration.

Ground rules
● Fish that are decorated with sequins, tissue paper, and so on cannot be used for the games because the decorations are likely to come off.
● When the children are racing their fish they cannot touch them with the newspaper.

Differentiation
This is easy and fun for younger children. They especially enjoy racing the fish and ejecting them from the parachute.

AGE RANGE 5–11

SUMMARY
Children make their own games to play.

Game designers

What you need
Copies of the 'Game designers (1) and (2)' photocopiable sheets on pages 94 and 95, copied onto card (enough for one per pair or group); colouring pens and pencils; scissors.

What to do
Less able or younger children

● Give each group a card copy of the 'Game designers (1)' photocopiable sheet. Tell the children to colour the squares on the grid and to draw snakes and ladders to link the lower and higher squares.
● Then explain that they need to cut out and colour the counters and number cards at the bottom of the sheet.
● To play the game without a dice, explain to the children that they should take turns to shuffle and lay the number cards face down. Each player takes a turn to select a card and this determines the number of spaces that they move their counter. Explain that they will need to reshuffle the cards each time they pick one up. Alternatively, they can put the number cards into a bag so they can't guess which number they can pick up.

More able or older children
● The children can work in pairs or small groups. Give each pair or group a card copy of the 'Game designers (2)' photocopiable sheet.
● Tell the children that they should decide on a theme for their game. This might be 'ocean world', 'detectives', 'pop stars', or based on a book or film.
● Encourage the children to decorate their board with appropriate illustrations for their theme and to colour it in. Suggest they design a title and draw or write it in the title scroll.
● Encourage them to think about board games that they enjoy playing and then compile a simple list of rules for the game.
● The children can use the counters and dice cards from the 'Game designers (1)' photocopiable sheet.
● Tell them that in the squares they can write instructions like 'Miss a turn' or 'Go back three spaces'.
● The children could use the first playtime to design and prepare the game. They can then play their own and each other's games in subsequent breaks in the day.

Differentiation
Encourage older children to add reasons for their board instructions in line with the theme of their game. The theme of Jane's game is a football club, so one of her squares might read: 'Scored a goal, move forward five spaces'.

AGE RANGE 5–11

SUMMARY
Children make treasure maps and hide their treasure for others to find.

Treasure maps

What you need
Copies of the 'Treasure maps' photocopiable sheet on page 96 (enough for one per child); colouring pens and pencils; a whiteboard or flipchart and writing materials; paper.

What to do
● Ask the children to suggest things that may be found on a treasure map. Write their answers on the board and add some of the following suggestions: woods, a well, caves, mountains, a ruined building, a river, a graveyard.
● Give each child a copy of the 'Treasure map' photocopiable sheet. Explain that they should draw their own island shape on the grid. Encourage them to add and colour in features from the list on the board to their treasure map. They also need to write their names at the top of the sheet.
● Next, tell them they have to decide where to hide their treasure. On a separate piece of paper they need to write their name, where they have hidden their treasure and the grid reference. These should be folded, given to the play leader and put into a sealed envelope.
● In pairs, or table groups of four to six, tell the children to look at each other's maps and guess where the treasure is.
● Explain that they can ask each other questions, such as *Is it near a tree? Is it south of the river? Is it near water?*
● Each child should have a piece of paper to write their name and the grid reference where they think the treasure is buried. For example, Lorna would write her name on her paper and *I think Simon's treasure is buried at B7*. If they are playing in table groups, the children should guess where the treasure is on all of the maps.
● Towards the end of the session, invite the children to take turns to say where the treasure is buried on the maps. The person whose map it was announces who guessed correctly.
● If nobody guessed correctly, they can tell the other players the answer and prove it by showing them the paper with their name and grid reference.

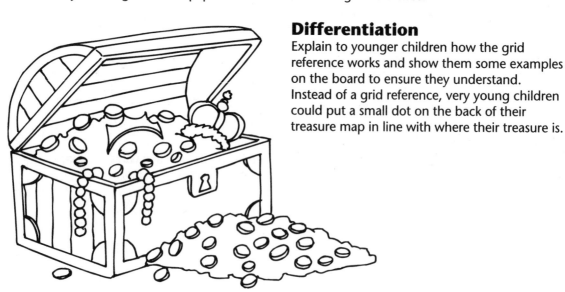

Differentiation
Explain to younger children how the grid reference works and show them some examples on the board to ensure they understand. Instead of a grid reference, very young children could put a small dot on the back of their treasure map in line with where their treasure is.

Whirly snakes

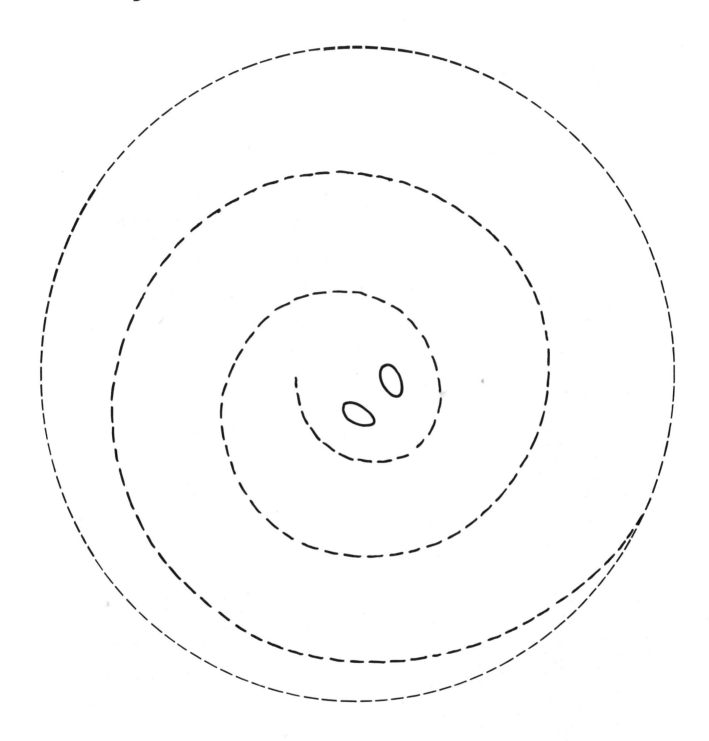

Spinners

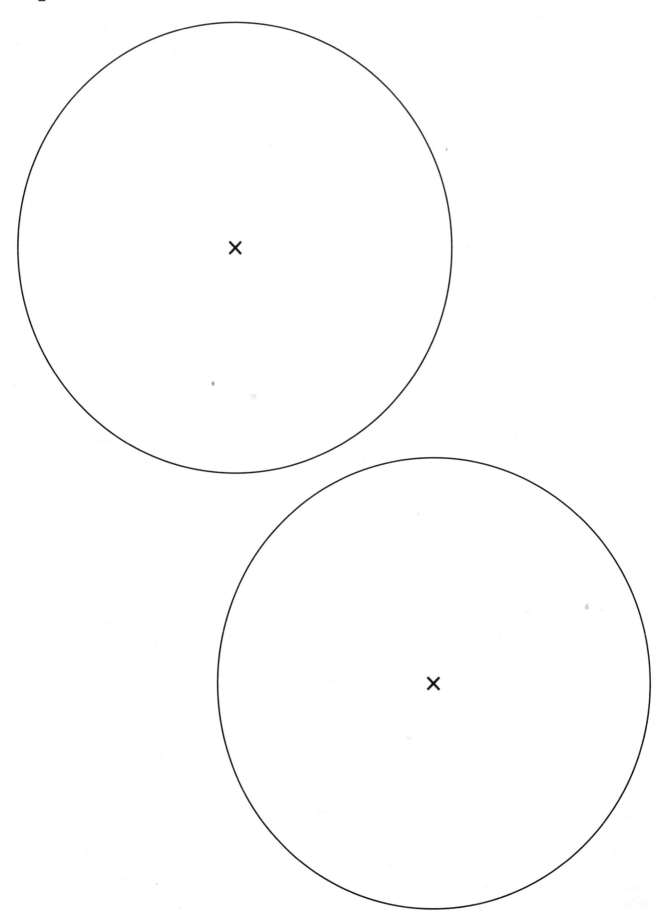

Wet Playtimes BRIGHT IDEAS

Freaky faces

SCHOLASTIC

Fashion show (1)

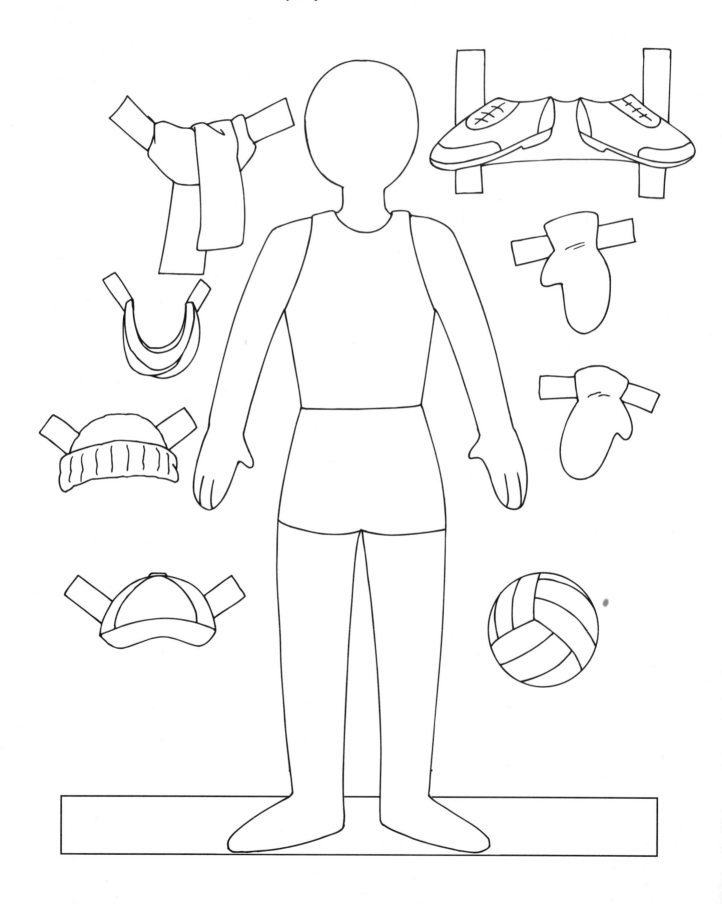

Wet Playtimes BRIGHT IDEAS

Fashion show (2)

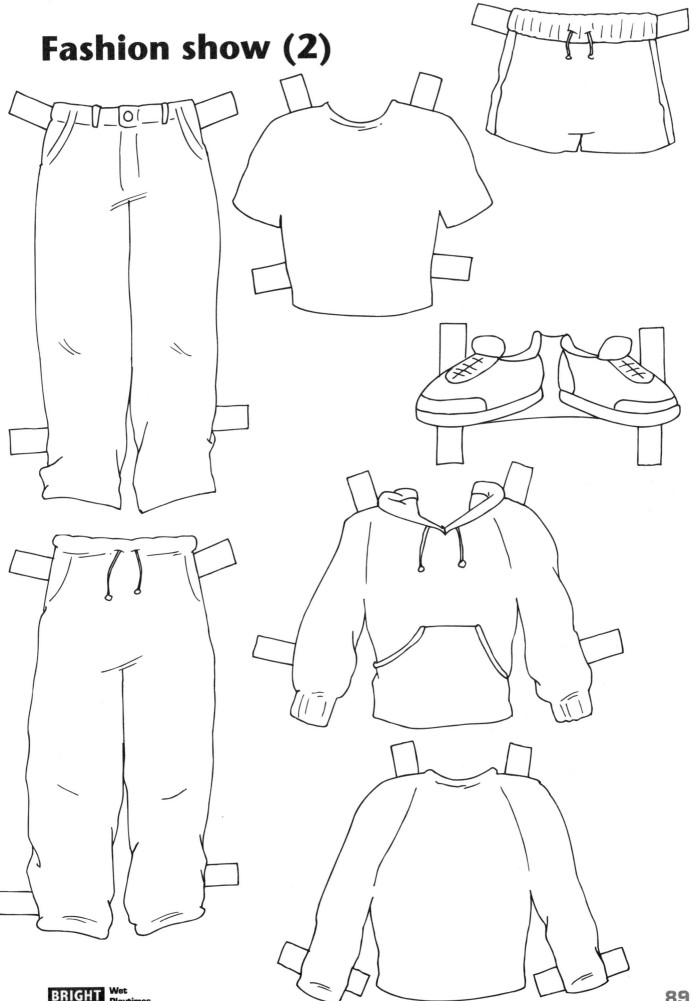

PHOTOCOPIABLE

◾SCHOLASTIC

Balloon people

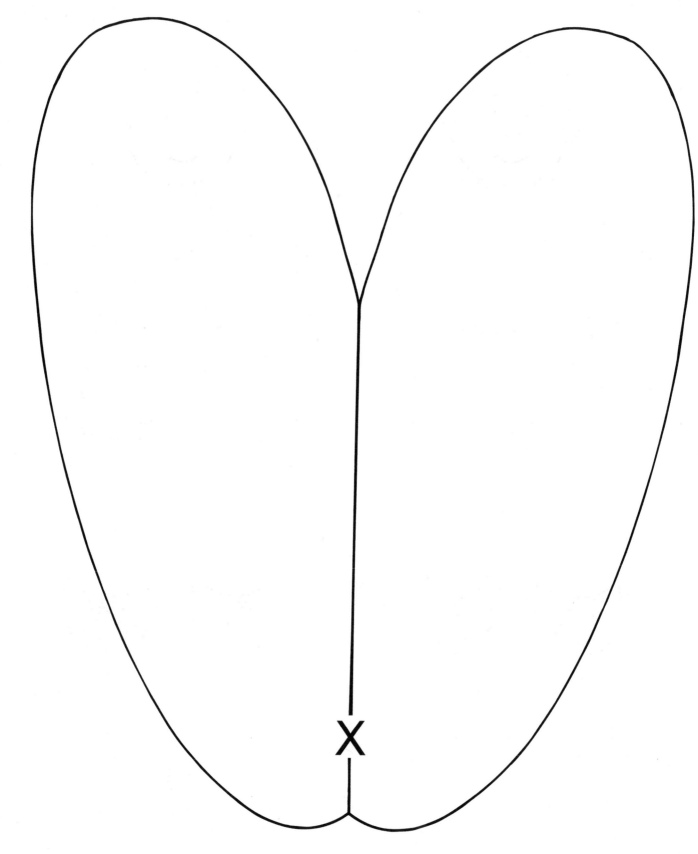

Wet
Playtimes BRIGHT IDEAS

Funny footballers

Spooky portraits

Wet Playtimes

BRIGHT IDEAS

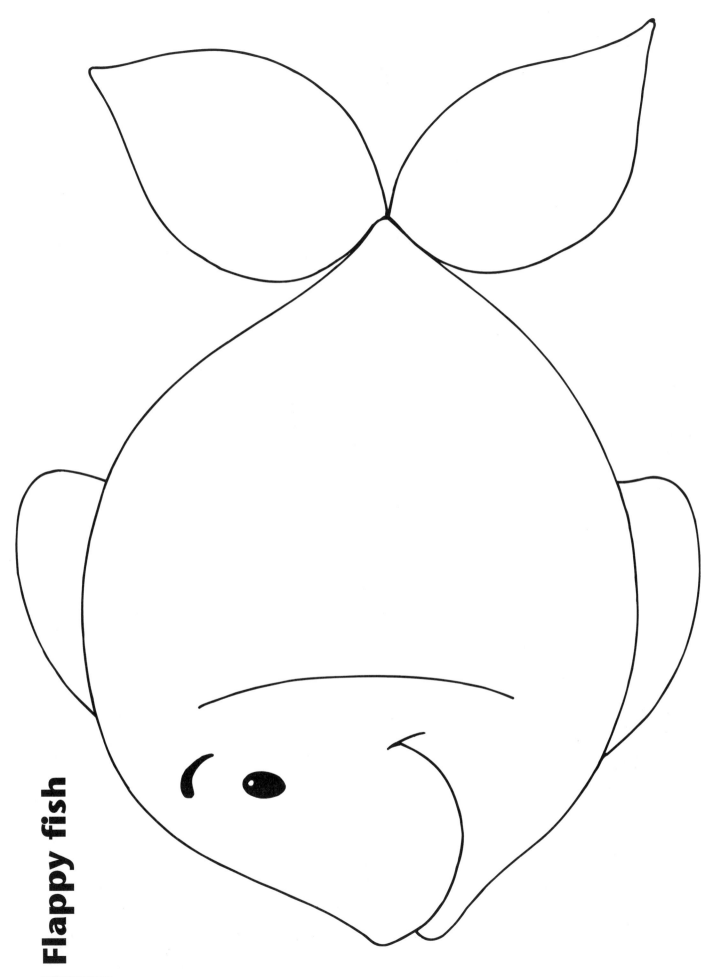

Flappy fish

📖SCHOLASTIC

Game designers (1)

Counters

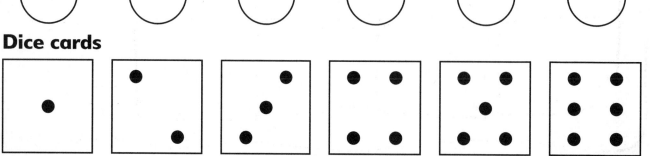

Dice cards

Wet
Playtimes   BRIGHT
IDEAS

PHOTOCOPIABLE

Game designers (2)

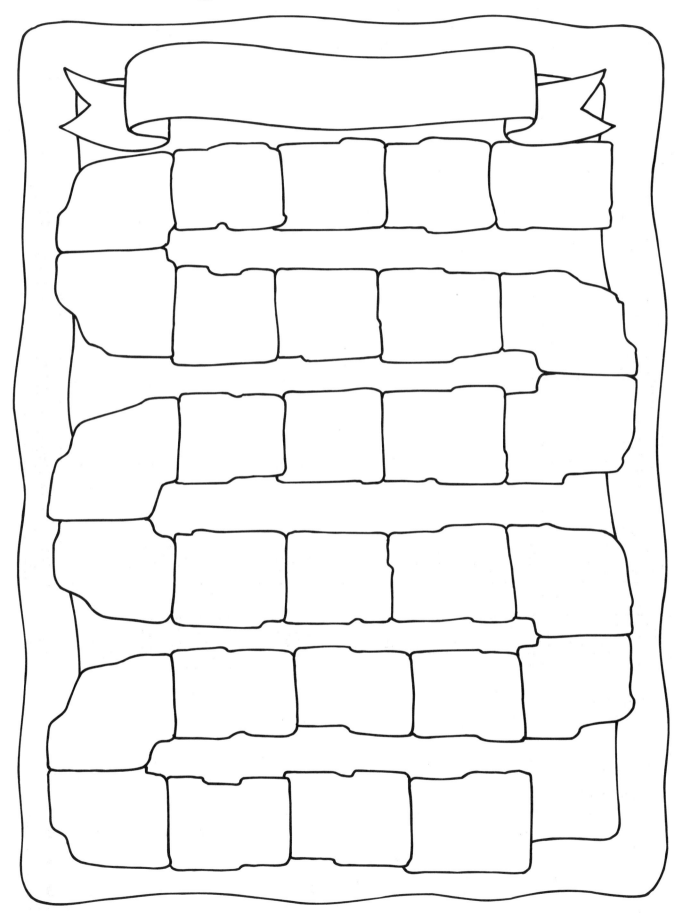

Treasure maps

	A	B	C	D	E	F	G	H	
1									1
2									2
3									3
4									4
5									5
6									6
7									7
8									8
	A	B	C	D	E	F	G	H	

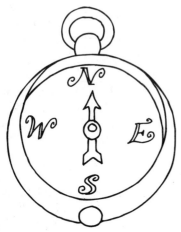

Wet Playtimes

BRIGHT IDEAS